Why you should read this book

"This book will disturb your emotions and thoughts, make you feel sorry or resentful, agree and disagree with the authors. That's exactly the process that parents should go through considering an adoption."

Boris Gindis, Ph.D.
Chief Psychologist
Center for Cognitive-Developmental Assessment and Remediation.
www.bgcenter.com

"An important contribution to the literature on attachment in adoption. This book provides a unique understanding of attachment issues by a highly regarded therapist with many years of experience in the adoption field. It offers reassurance and specific solutions for building attachment in adoptive families."

Connie Mancini Haack, LCSW
Adoption Social Worker and Home Study Specialist.
www.nyhomestudy.com

If I Love My Kid Enough

If I Love My Kid Enough

✦

The Reality of Raising An Adopted Child

Sara-Jane Hardman
Jean Roe Mauro, LCSW

iUniverse, Inc.
New York Lincoln Shanghai

If I Love My Kid Enough
The Reality of Raising An Adopted Child

iUniverse books may be ordered through booksellers or by contacting:

iUniverse
2021 Pine Lake Road, Suite 100
Lincoln, NE 68512
www.iuniverse.com
1-800-Authors (1-800-288-4677)

Because of the dynamic nature of the Internet, any Web addresses or links contained in this book may have changed since publication and may no longer be valid.

The views expressed in this work are solely those of the author and do not necessarily reflect the views of the publisher, and the publisher hereby disclaims any responsibility for them.

ISBN: 978-0-595-46194-3 (pbk)
ISBN: 978-0-595-90494-5 (ebk)

Printed in the United States of America

In memory of Janelle Peterson whose clear and compelling voice encouraged us to explore and understand *The Invisible Road* walked by adoptive parents.

Contents

ACKNOWLEDGEMENTS

Thank you to:

Our children who showed interest and encouragement all the way through. Even when they found it difficult to revisit those years, they understood our need for completing the task.

Peter for his encouragement and confidence.

Connie Haack who participated in many ways too numerous to mention in order to encourage and support the message.

Anne Kimble Loux, Renee Lowden, Susan Jeffers, Jerry Kurtz for their early ideas and encouragement.

Ellen Foreman, Judith Harrison, Elaine Robbins, Miriam Tarplin, Marcie Woodruff and Linda Zelizer, our earliest readers who gave their time and shared their insights.

Arzi Mckeown whose creativity, time and energy helped keep the fire lit.

Former student Effie Sentouktsi who as a responsive reader and creative thinker shared her own stories and reassured us that the story was worth telling.

Cathy Cioffi and Little Heart for the graphic design.

And to Ellen Joseph for being there from start to finish with her unique contributions as editor, motivator and partner.

Note: Names in the narrative and some of the minor details have been changed to protect the people involved.

INTRODUCTION

When Bethany came into our family she was the answer to our prayers—bright, beautiful, and irresistible. My husband John and I could not believe the good fortune that united our adoptive son with his biological sister and completed our vision for our family. But from the beginning, there were indications that this might not be a happily-ever-after story.

In spite of her potential and all of our love, we saw small concerns and issues that we had noted in Bethany's early years magnified as she moved into her adolescence. We watched her develop into a teenager with whirlwind behaviors who was self-centered and unfocused, with a poorly developed conscience and no goals for her future. She refused to go to school, abused drugs, and developed troubled relationships.

We were unprepared to provide the parenting Bethany needed as she moved through childhood and into the challenges of the teen years. The standard responses such as providing intellectual and athletic challenges, rewards, punishments, individual and group therapy, family counseling, and hospitalizations had no effect.

As we worked to control Bethany's behavior and maintain our family unity, we searched through libraries, schools, professional offices, community resources, and a variety of therapeutic programs. All proved to be ineffectual. The force of Bethany's reaction to her circumstances and the ineffectiveness of the solutions used to help her were bewildering. Many adoptive parents experience this bewilderment as their children develop unexpected behaviors that are unresponsive to attention. They do not know how to understand their child's actions or how best to parent under these circumstances.

The face of adoption has changed dramatically in the last twenty years. Recent research has uncovered substantial issues that are just now being identified and understood by professionals whose practices have been shaped by the number of challenged adoptive families seeking help. With the popularity of street and designer drugs come hundreds of thousands of babies born with addictions. Some children, having suffered instability and abuse in their lives prior to adoption, present another set of problems. The common practice internationally of housing babies in orphanages where they are affected by inconsistent nurturing, and in this country, of moving children from one foster home to another, even in their earliest days, leaves them emotionally vulnerable.

But to our knowledge Bethany experienced none of these early traumas. To the contrary, John and I were told that Bethany had been in one secure foster home from birth, and her life had been free of early adversity. Yet despite our well intentioned love and healthy models, Bethany developed anti-social behaviors that were untreatable with standard therapies. She was an apparently normal child, with no known genetic problems and no known history of abuse or neglect who turned into a dysfunctional and self-destructive person once she hit adolescence.

We know that early experiences contribute significantly to each child's specific developmental picture. Genetics, prenatal influences, early or multiple separations in the first year of life, and difficulties in bonding with new parents all play a considerable part in establishing what the child will need as her development proceeds. Mild to severe attachment issues can develop. In Bethany's case, her unique history involved two painful experiences with separation by the age of seven months. A third bonding did not come naturally to her. She needed help to reestablish lost trust and attach to her adoptive mother.

Bethany's story is one among many based on the themes of separation, loss and attachment. Attachment is a necessary emotional dependence on the mother that is critical to the child's survival and future development. Parents can familiarize themselves with her experience and understand the principles involved in the dynamics of her adoption and all adoptions. If parents can understand from the earliest days the part separation plays in each child's development, the less confusing parenting will be. Parenting preparation is necessary in other areas as well, for very important reasons. Adoptive parents often do not know whether the expectations they hold for their child's development are realistic. Since they often have little knowledge of the child's genetic background or of the prenatal experiences of mother and child, they do not have the intuitive sense of the child that they might have if they had given birth to her. It is best if adoptive parents can receive as much specific information about their children as possible, in order to understand their child's developmental progress from conception to the time of placement. They can then start out with informed, realistic expectations that will give their children the best chance for success.

Our endeavors to find help were frustrating and painful, and flew in the face of the popularly held belief that even if the journey was difficult, love would be enough. The therapists with whom we consulted could not help us pinpoint any issues in the family that might have caused Bethany's struggles, nor could they help us understand what else was responsible. A lot of time was wasted on our personal feelings of guilt and inadequacy. We know now that this was pointless. We could not have prevented any of the behaviors that caused us all so much anguish. We did not create the problems and love alone could not have corrected them.

The experience of adoption requires extraordinary diligence from parents at every stage. In early years, parents must steadfastly work to adopt their children. Dealing with infertility, costly and exotic medical procedures, bureaucracies, the legal system, intrusive questions are only a part of the job. They then must show a single-minded dedication as they challenge the standard jargon of therapists, school systems, and well-intentioned friends in their search to find the best information and treatments. With time and experience, we have come to understand that the common diagnoses of oppositional defiance and other conduct disorders which are assigned to teenagers in turmoil are not adequate for evaluating our children and not helpful in understanding their behaviors.

Current research gives us answers to many of our questions. Various treatments reflecting this new knowledge have been developed to help every adoptive family whose children reflect a range of early life experiences and prenatal influences that other children do not have.

When John and I were going through many of our problems with Bethany, we turned to Jean Roe Mauro, LCSW, a psychotherapist, adoptive parent, and member of our adoptive parent support group. Jean had seen many families like ours in her years of practice. Her own children were also living with significant challenges. She knew that there were no easy answers and that there was scant knowledge readily available to most parents. Together we looked for a suitable educational and therapeutic program for Bethany while also researching new diagnoses and treatments that might be helpful for us in understanding and directing her.

We are writing this book for adoptive parents, perspective adoptive parents, and professionals working in the field of adoption and child development. Guidelines are provided for receiving support from others and for learning the specific parenting skills needed.

As attachment theory has become more widely accepted it has become clear that children who are not adopted can and sometimes do exhibit some of the same characteristics displayed by Bethany. These children may have been through some similar early life experiences which inhibit healthy attachments. For adopted children, the reliable constant in the developmental picture is that there is always a separation from the first mother, and there is always the necessity of bonding to a new mother in order for attachment to take place. This is an added developmental step for the child that requires attention and understanding.

This book, the result of our collaboration, describes what it can mean to be an adoptive parent today. We have divided each chapter into two narratives. The first voice in each chapter is a description of Bethany's development from infancy to adolescence with emphasis on the behaviors that caused so much concern. The second voice is Jean's and provides an explanation for these behaviors by contrasting normal development with that of the child whose early experiences have necessitated the severing of the first attachment from the birthmother. It describes the child's struggle to reattach to another caregiver and perhaps even another. The book discusses recent research and the latest effective treatments and available resources while giving encouragement in making decisions that are difficult, but unavoidable.

During that euphoric time, when your child first comes home and you are enthralled with her presence, it will be difficult to imagine the challenges that may arise. It is almost inconceivable to picture what can happen to this child in her teens. Yet, what we describe here does happen in many more adoptive homes than has been previously realized.

We learned many things throughout our years of parenting Bethany. We learned new strategies for parenting. We learned to be more flexible with our expectations and never to give up on her by continuing to seek resources and additional tools for helping her find her way. The most important qualities we possessed as parents throughout these years were commitment, persistence, and patience. Although it was a struggle, we found many rewards to celebrate along the way as Bethany reached each new stage of growth. Eventually, she accomplished significant gains in attachment and completed the journey to becoming a mature adult.

The source of our children's difficulties may ultimately remain a mystery. We do not have complete records and complete histories. But now that we have research available on the very earliest stages of development, we can concentrate our efforts on optimizing early attachment so that they can ultimately become the mature, responsible, and honest adults they need to be.

1

JUST ONE STORY

"It was our family miracle and we could not contain our joy."

The phone call came at about 4:30 on a Sunday afternoon. It could have been worse. For months I had imagined the one that would come in the middle of the night, the one that would tell me of a young girl's body recovered from the East River or a garbage dumpster, or it might inform me that my sixteen year old daughter had been arrested and was being held at the county jail. But this caller just asked if I had recently authorized anyone to use my Visa card.

In slow motion, I had watched a steady progression of destructive behaviors: illegal absences from school, disappearances from home, unexplained clothing acquisitions, piles of trash accumulating in her bedroom, phone calls at 3:00 in the morning from unfamiliar young men, unprovoked arguments, unpredictable rages—now the credit cards. It seemed like we had reached a new level of defiance and there were no good solutions available.

Through the years I had noted the headlines and talk shows that focused on the stories of children out of control. As an adoptive parent, I reluctantly paid particular attention to those that involved adoptees. Too often they focused on notorious criminals who were represented by lawyers attesting to the circumstances of their adoptions, "adoption rage," as one defender called it. But I dismissed these as gross exaggerations by a sensationalist press and comforted myself with the knowledge that my child had been loved and nurtured from early infancy, that adoption was not a hidden subject in our home and that we who had such control over our own lives would not be blindsided when our children encountered the confusing adolescent years. Yet, now it had come to this, a phone call from a stranger telling me that there had been a lot of unusual activity on my credit card.

Numerous "experts" had told us that Bethany would have to hit bottom before she could turn her life around. But where was the bottom? It wasn't when she had failed every subject in her second year of high school. It wasn't when she

1

found herself in a remote location on the bottom of a pile of drunken adolescent boys. It wasn't when she was thrown out of her second high school, the one with a "suitable therapeutic program," geared to her needs. How low could we go before she hit the bottom? I dared my imagination to reach that point and tortured myself with the mental images I could not avoid of violent encounters between her and various criminals or of her lying in a hospital bed permanently attached to tubes. My imagination knew no limits. I slept little at night, pacing, fretting and waiting for the phone to ring.

How had we arrived at this point? Clearly, Bethany was not reacting to violence and abuse at home. She was not living in a dysfunctional family. Was her behavior a response to cultural insanity encouraged by the media and her contemporaries whose unprecedented freedoms knew no bounds? And why was she like this and not like the thousands of other teenagers including her brother Matthew who still went to school everyday, joined academic and athletic programs and set their sights on college and successful careers in spite of the immorality reflected in our culture? What had we missed? What might my husband and I have done to redirect the present course that her life was taking?

Over and over my mind switched from the present turmoil back to the early years when all was possible and Bethany's presence was a sign of limitless hope and potential. It was hard to see how we had arrived at these present days of disaster. Ours was a romantic adoption story involving sadness, frustration, disappointment and ultimately glorious triumph.

When a child enters a family through adoption it is most often the end of a long and arduous trial and the arrival of this child feels just right. In our case, we had endured years of infertility, painful and futile testing, four miscarriages, raised hopes and exploding dreams. I gloomily observed the easy pregnancies of friends and strangers and, as a middle school teacher, I watched as twelve-year-old children became pregnant without a single thought, while I consulted doctors from a variety of trainings, absorbed harmful and ultimately useless drugs, charted my temperature, faced east, scheduled lovemaking trysts, etc. etc. etc. Meanwhile, time proceeded inevitably on. From the day that my husband, John, and I said those wonderful words, "Let's have a baby," until our first child entered our home, seven painful and frustrating years had passed.

Adoptive parents tell wonderful stories. They speak of courage and perseverance, sadness and desperation, hope, and renewal. In our case, we treasured the arrival of our son, Matthew, who was beautiful and bright, a delightful child, and we wanted him to have a sibling. So knowing what lay ahead, we began our search early on for a second baby. We went the now familiar route. We contacted agencies. We placed ads, installed a separate phone line, jumped every time it rang, talked to endless young women and then out of the blue got a phone call that a baby was due in three months. If we would agree to help support the mother for a short while the child could be ours. We did agree and began faithfully sending our checks to Amanda every week until the final days of the pregnancy when she was due in New York to deliver our child.

A beautiful sunny day, our lawyer awaits a pregnant woman at La Guardia airport. We have by this time taught Matthew to wash his little baby doll and talk to it and tell it stories to prepare him for the new baby. The plane lands. Amanda is not on board, nor is she on the next two flights from Cleveland. Frantic phone calls confirmed that she was not in her apartment back home nor was she delivering prematurely in any of the Cleveland hospitals that we called. No explanation, no apology, nothing. She and her baby had disappeared.

We were all devastated. It was a familiar sour adoption experience retold by countless disappointed families. After three months of following Amanda's pregnancy and helping to support her, she disappeared. We tried unsuccessfully to track her down, but calls to her doctor and her landlord led nowhere. Heartbroken, feeling betrayed and stupid, we could not make the hurt go away. When a month later she resurfaced having changed her mind again, we were too wary to reestablish the relationship.

Skip ahead two months. The phone rings. It is the caseworker who placed Matthew with us. "Please come into the office. There is something I want to discuss with you." I knew. My intuition told me that Matt's birthmother had had another baby and, as with the first pregnancy, she was unable to keep this child. We had a weekend to think about the upcoming meeting and the anticipation was excruciating. But Monday morning finally arrived, and there we were sitting in this tiny cubicle, hearing about Matthew's baby sister and silently screaming with renewed and soaring hope.

The timing was perfect. We were ecstatic. This had to be another perfect baby. After all, we reasoned, she had the same genes as our beautiful son. And how wonderful for him to have his biological sister in his life! What would have happened if we had gotten that other baby? Could we have also said yes to welcoming Bethany? It was our family miracle and we could not contain our joy.

No fairy tale could have had a happier ending. This beautiful little girl, "The best and most alert baby I ever took care of," according to her foster mother, was to join our family at the age of seven months. This must be our reward for all the difficulties that we had endured.

◆   ◆   ◆

Sara and John struggled through a long and painful preparation for adoptive parenthood, a story familiar to many adoptive families. First they had the wish to have a child, then they attempted to become pregnant. Eventually, with the recognition of infertility, they made the decision to turn towards adoption as a resolution to the desire to have a family.

Having decided to adopt, Sara and John did not find this a quick, smooth, or easy process. Most parents or potential adoptive parents today recognize and understand the feeling of insecurity about whether they will actually be successful at having children and becoming a family. The news that a child is on the way is overwhelming and hard to trust after so many false starts, high hopes, and letdowns, It is also full of wonder, gratitude and joy.

Within this framework, it is difficult to remain focused on the realities of adoptive parenthood. And yet, that is exactly what would be of most benefit to adoptive parents and their children. Workshops or seminars to prepare parents for what to expect and how best to parent each individual child could provide grounding for the new family. This form of preparation is still not readily available in many areas but could be sought out through local adoption support groups or other professionals working in the field of adoption such as lawyers, social workers, psychologists, psychiatrists or educators.

New developmental research by professionals such as Janelle Peterson and Nancy Verrier is now available that offers information about how to understand the importance of the prenatal experience, the history of each child up to the time she comes home and any genetic factors that can be obtained from the birthmother. Much of this information may be hard to find, since an understanding of its importance is relatively new. Yet, informed parents can put effort into gathering all the information they possibly can in order to understand their child when they bring her home. They can learn how to prepare themselves for what their child will need most from them by becoming familiar with the stages of child development from prenatal experience on and by becoming attuned to their child's body language and reactions to daily life experiences. They can also become comfortable with the idea of using support from family and friends. They can search out professional help in the community as they parent in order to give their children the best chance for healthy growth and success.

As Sara said, Bethany's story is just one story, just one version of the adoption experience. In many respects, it is very different from her brother Matt's story and different from the stories of many other adoptive children. Yet, the dynamics of adoption remain the same for all and can be applied to daily life experiences to aid in understanding how issues of attachment apply to each individual child and what the effects are on normal developmental processes. Some children affected by attachment issues may have poor motivation, difficulty socializing, learning disabilities or ADD. They may appear to be overly shy and display behaviors associated with lack of assertiveness. Many will not have the devastating effects of Bethany's early life experiences due to different histories and different genetics. Yet all adoptive parents can understand their children better and parent them more successfully if they are fully prepared for their parenting roles and have an informed idea of what to expect.

2

BEFORE THE BEGINNING: THE UNEASY WOMB

"Mommy, why does Barbara cry so much?" Bethany would ask.

How does one prepare for the arrival of a new baby? The pregnant mother feels the early fluttering in her womb. Mother and child are quickly connected in the most intimate of physical and emotional relationships that two human beings can have. They are locked together, united with every breath and every movement. Lovingly, the expectant mother holds her belly, symbolically cradling the new life. She hums to the baby, talks to her, strokes her. In her daily life, she is concerned for her child's diet, protecting her from harmful substances and joyfully planning for the day when she will deliver a healthy child who will continue to feel her protection and love.

I had never carried a pregnancy to term, but I had had several pregnancies that ended in spontaneous abortions. Although of short duration, those pregnancies, long sought and long imagined, were an exciting part of my life, and each time I became pregnant my state of mind would change significantly. I would go into fantasy mode imagining my baby's life and the impact it would have on our family and our lives together. Lying in bed, my mind would quickly skirt from looking for the changes in my body, to cuddling with my baby and carrying her in my arms. I would picture our family's fairy tale existence together, watching her move into the bright future that I imagined. I would do what I assume most prospective parents do and plan how I could enrich her life until she was perfectly prepared for her adulthood. Yet now that my dream was changing, I tried to imagine what it would be like for a woman who was planning to give her baby away. What would she be thinking and experiencing and how would this affect her child? I did a lot of research on the subject of prenatal life and learned a great deal about what it must be like for a birthmother who does not plan to keep her baby.

What I learned was extensive. For the baby who is going to be placed for adoption this early experience may be very different. Often overwhelmed by her circumstances, the young mother cannot afford the luxury of bonding, for if she becomes too close to the life that is growing inside of her, separation will be even more difficult. Though physically united, the birthmother may remain emotionally detached, aware that at the end of their nine months together they will be divided forever. So she does little to comfort and caress her baby, makes no plans for its future and tries not to imagine its daily development. In order to protect herself from the pain of a broken attachment, she will stay as unconnected as possible, depriving the growing fetus of the sense of oneness that she needs in order to build a base for trust. The uterus, which should be a nurturing and healthful environment, instead becomes a source of discomfort and stress for the baby, setting the stage for an uneasy development.

As a result, at birth, Bethany, like many adopted children, is already vulnerable. Now she will have to adjust to a completely new world without the familiar set of sounds, smells, and feelings she has become used to in utero, without the mother who has provided her with her tenuous first nurturing and without the ability to understand or even question what is happening.

Where does this leave the adoptive family? In our ignorance, we hadn't given much thought to this or to how it would affect our child's life. As the new parents, we had been denied the earliest contacts. We had to content ourselves with planning for the baby's life at a period after birth while hoping that a fifteen year old was mature and wise enough to take good care of our unborn child, thus minimizing the effects of the unwanted pregnancy.

Over the years, I would avoid conversations with other mothers when the subject of pregnancies was brought up. It was too painful to me to think about what I had missed and besides, I really couldn't do anything about it. I couldn't dwell on the secret that I kept, which was that Bethany and Matt's birthmother had denied both of her pregnancies and had done nothing to get prenatal care. Both children, though full term, had weighed less than six pounds at birth, and in both cases, the birthmother had made no plans for their placement until after their arrival.

So, I surprised myself when the children were very young by agreeing to bring birthmothers into our home. As active members of an adoption support group, John and I were asked to provide a home for pregnant women while they awaited the birth of their babies. Weighing the pros and cons of the request, we reasoned that it would help our children understand that birthmothers were real, not just people to be fantasized about, and that the decision to give up a child was not an easy one. Mothers did not just casually toss their babies out when things got diffi-cult. On two occasions, we opened our home to two women. Our relationships with the young women lasted only a few weeks, but in that short time they were very intimate.

My heart went out to them as they told me about their lives. They were intel-ligent young women. They were caring and thoughtful and grateful for the sup-port and attention. I wanted them to feel comfortable so that their unhappiness was lessened. I also wanted them to have healthy and happy babies that could grow up in secure homes, as did they. I wanted them to build their own lives so that they could have promising futures, and I also wished that things were differ-ent and that they could keep their babies. Unfortunately, their circumstances were too difficult.

I became a surrogate mother providing the role of confidant and confessor. I also monitored their diets, cooked healthy meals, and encouraged them to take walks while I praised them for refraining from smoking and drinking. But mostly, I tried to keep their spirits up, for them and for their babies. All the while they were there, my mind would slide over to Bethany's and Matt's birthmother wondering if she had anyone to listen to her and help her bring healthy babies into the world. She had been in her teens when they were born. These women were older. Though they had more life experiences to rely on, they shared many problems too. Early on, they had denied their pregnancies. Afraid to tell their families, boyfriends or the men who had abused them, they did not seek prenatal care nor find comfort in their relationships. What should have been a time for optimism and happiness was instead a source of unrelenting stress, highlighting the glaring inadequacies of their relationships and the precariousness of their young lives. Every day of the early pregnancy was spent wishing it didn't exist and maintaining a distance from the developing fetus as they impatiently awaited the day when it was over and they could resume their own unfulfilled lives.

While Matt did not interact much with the young women, Bethany was more involved. She would talk to them. They would paint each other's toenails, fix each other's hair, put on makeup and do girlie kinds of things. Both of the women were honest and caring, but both were as needy for attention as our own children and would talk endlessly of their present predicament. Conflicted over their concern for their own and their babies' futures, they spent hours crying over their decisions and the status of their lives. "Mommy, why does Barbara cry so much?" Bethany would ask.

How unnatural all of this is! Nature and society tell these young women they must love their babies unconditionally, but reality warns them against doing so.

Under normal circumstances, this should be the happiest time of their lives, but it is just the opposite. How distressing it must be!

In our blissful ignorance, we didn't give much thought to the circumstances of Bethany's birth or to how these circumstances would affect her life. In hindsight, we would say, we did not know what we did not know. We were confident that love would be enough to overcome any hurdles that we encountered.

◆   ◆   ◆

Unlike most adoptive parents, Sara had the unique experience of caring for birthmothers in her home. Her family could see first hand how much suffering is involved in the momentous decision to give up a child. All the birthmothers I have worked with professionally have been sad and tearful. They find themselves grieving before and after the birth. Some have denied their condition up until the last month or two before birth, continuing with their usual activities and pretending to themselves and to others that there is no pregnancy. Others have been careful about their health and deliberate in making plans for the baby's future. Frequently, they discuss an adoption plan with a lawyer. Sometimes they know and work with the potential adoptive family. They may ask for therapeutic services for themselves so they can talk out their feelings about this very important event in their lives. There is a wide range of circumstances between these two extremes of denial and careful planning.

The extent of the birthfather's involvement also varies greatly. Sometimes he is involved and wants to be a part of the process of choosing an adoptive family. Occasionally, the birthfather is unknown, a chance encounter resulting in pregnancy, while the birthmother has a close relationship with another man to whom she plans to return after the baby's birth and placement. Sometimes the birthfather is still around, but chooses to reject the birthmother and refuses to acknowledge the pregnancy. The circumstances of the relationship that resulted in pregnancy have a profound effect on the mother while she is carrying the child, almost always resulting in a sense of abandonment and failure.

Pregnancy alters every aspect of a woman's life, creating the environment in which the developing fetus will grow. Her physical well being, as well as her state of mind, are key to the baby's development. How does she feel about being pregnant? How do those around her feel? Does society approve? Is she in love with the father of the baby? Is she physically healthy and drug and alcohol free? Is she stable and supported in her home life, allowing her to concentrate on this intimate experience? Will the baby be provided the opportunities for a rich and productive life?

The cycle of life is assured by the processes of conception, pregnancy, and birth. The hope is always that the pregnancy is welcomed and has resulted from a loving relationship, that the period of gestation will be full term and provide intense bonding between mother and child and that the new life will be healthy. In order for bonding to take place, nature demands that the mother turn inward, focusing her emotions and attentions on the growing fetus (Brazelton and Cramer 1974).

In the best of pregnancies, there are emotional ups and downs with concern and even worry about the developing fetus. Mixed with their fears, pregnant women fantasize about the baby, much as Sara did, dreaming about her arrival and the pleasure of holding, rocking, and feeding this new life that is being nurtured and protected in the womb. Turning inward takes place automatically as a necessary part of the bonding experience.

According to Brazelton, the mother feels the first stirrings of the baby somewhere in the fifth month of the pregnancy. This bonding will then continue to develop into a unique and evermore complex relationship until the moment of birth. What happens during these months will set the stage for the drama that will play out during the rest of the baby's life. In addition to the emotional implications, there are concerns for the physical and mental attributes that will be passed on. The genetic makeup of the parents, combined with their health at the time of conception, will determine the constitution of the baby.

When the birthmother cannot keep and raise her baby, complications arise to threaten the basic health of the growing fetus. The mother who did not consciously intend to become pregnant and who has decided she cannot keep her baby, or is struggling with what to do after her baby is born will have a strained pregnancy. She usually does not have a solid support system and is feeling anxious about her own well being. She has made the commitment to carry the baby to term, but she does not have the freedom emotionally to love the baby, be happy about the impending birth or look forward to holding, feeding and nurturing her infant. Often the young woman is frightened and angry about her circumstances while simultaneously suffering from the loss of the relationship with the birthfather and her sense of security in her own family. If she is confused and anxious, conditions exist for her child to be born with attachment issues. Among the many factors affecting this problem are a denial of the pregnancy, a rejection of the fetus, substance abuse, inadequate prenatal maternal care and the physical immaturity so common in teenage mothers. In some cases where children are born outside of the US, conditions of extreme poverty and societal upheaval compound the problem. The consequence is that trust does not usually develop in the womb. Instead, the birthmother is only partially bonding and connecting to her child. The baby is to a greater or lesser degree left to develop in an isolated world. Later, many of these children describe themselves as islands, separated from meaningful human connections.

Throughout pregnancy, the fetus is being shaped by the experiences of the mother. Medical science is now engaged in monitoring fetal movements and heart rates, and there is confirmation that the fetus is responding to what goes on outside the womb. At about the fifth month of pregnancy a communication system begins to develop between mother and fetus, and it becomes more complex as the pregnancy moves toward birth. Each day the fetus becomes increasingly aware of its surroundings.

According to noted pediatrician, T. Berry Brazelton, by the third trimester the fetus will respond to light, sound and touch. The fetus moves in synchronicity with the mother as the mother moves, walks or runs. The activity that the fetus is engaged in gives the mother feedback, telling her how the baby is reacting, even giving her a sense of what kind of person she is carrying. The attentive mother can tell that the fetus is sharing her experiences.

While the birthmother is continually learning about her developing child, recent research shows that the unborn child is already learning in the womb. Newborns recognize and react to music they were exposed to in utero, and it has been proven that after birth, babies recognize their mother's voice and her breast from its unique smell. Even childhood eating habits are learned in the womb as babies show strong preferences for foods their mothers ate during the pregnancy (Brazelton 1992, 28).

Since the developing fetus is so exquisitely attuned to the nuances of what is happening inside and outside the womb, the circumstances of an unsupported pregnancy will shape and focus the direction the baby will take after birth.

The physical health of the birthmother, determined by her diet, lifestyle and emotional state during pregnancy as well as the health of the birthfather at the time of conception will significantly affect the life of the growing child. Brazelton also tells us that if the mother suffers from malnutrition it can interfere with the development of as much as 40 percent of the cells in the fetal brain. If the birthmother is a teenager or if she is abusing substances, there is a serious risk of premature birth. Delivery can occur as much as three to four weeks early. Premature birth compromises the health of the developing organs and/or brain and central nervous system and results in an immature nervous system. Much of this damage may be long term or permanent, appearing after birth as a variety of conditions. Learning disabilities may emerge as the child develops which can cause problems including eventual difficulties in the school setting. As demands are made on the child's intellectual ability, the sense of apathy that marks the child with fetal alcohol syndrome will surface if alcohol has been abused by either parent.

Another possible complication of an unhealthy pregnancy is the interference with the formation of the myelin sheath which protects nerve cells and nerve endings. Without this protection, nerve cells are more exposed to physiological trauma and immature growth. In fact, Janelle Peterson, founder of Loving Homes, a child placement agency specializing in the placement of children with special needs, and author of *Can Do! Compendium on Post-Legal Adoption Issues* (1998) emphasizes the significance of the sheath in developing a healthy brain. She points to a possible link between Attention Deficit Hyperactivity Disorder (ADHD) and the absence of sufficient myelin protection (Peterson 1998, 5). The most crucial aspect of this effect on the growing fetus is that it is not possible for nerve cells to regenerate once they are affected.

Trauma to the fetus may also alter endorphin levels. These proteins that are produced by the pituitary gland, affect mood, pain perception, and provide a sense of satisfaction or joy. Normal neurological functioning results in extra endorphins being secreted during times of physical pain or stress. If the fetus experiences undue stress, the baby will be born with high levels of endorphins in her body possibly influencing later behavior.

As stated earlier, alcohol and drugs seriously affect the baby's health in utero. While it is obvious that hard drugs ingested during the critical phases of the pregnancy cut down on the complexity and number of brain cells in the fetus, it has now become apparent that drug use even at the time of conception, may cause neurological changes.

How significant are these issues when considering adoption? The reality, according to Peterson, is that today it is commonly recognized that a substance exposed infant is born about every 90 seconds. It is estimated that at least 62 percent of the population of current foster care and special needs adoptions has been affected by fetal alcohol exposure (Peterson 1998, 5).

In the 1980s, the number of children affected by prenatal substance abuse rose significantly due to the appearance of new street and designer drugs and rising alcohol use by adolescents and young adults. Many of these children upon reaching late adolescence went on to duplicate the cycle of substance abuse that occurred in their birth families, producing a new generation of babies with neurological and physiological difficulties.

Current statistics tell us that every year in America between 554,000 and 759,000 newborns are exposed to drugs or alcohol prior to birth. (Peterson 1998, 5) Babies who will be adopted also have the direct effect of a difficult in utero climate on bonding ability and developing personality. The deviations from a normal course of birth and in utero bonding will have long term effects on the child's ability to be responsive to adoptive parents.

In the majority of adoptions taking place in this country, eager parents rarely get substantial information about the children they hope to adopt. Whether the children are born domestically or internationally, they are often placed with incomplete and inaccurate records by lawyers, agencies and child care professionals who do not have in depth knowledge of neonatal development or background information about the children, thereby placing children and their parents in a position to experience years of confusion, anguish and self-blame if problems surface.

The commitment adoptive families make to parenting is far more challenging and difficult than conventional child rearing implies. Special effort is necessary in order to compensate for the gaps that exist in adoptive parents' knowledge of their children's histories. To fill the gaps, it is recommended that parents prepare themselves with the latest in neonatal and child development information that is available.

The rewards of adoption are considerable, but frequently they are hard won. It is essential that preparedness, determination and patience be balanced with the love that parents are eager to share.

3

THE FIRST YEAR: FORMING AN ATTACHMENT

"She wore this sad expression on her face as if she was mourning the loss of her best friend."

Bethany was already seven months old when we adopted her. We had missed the earliest stages of her development: when she picked up her head, her first smile, the day she started to crawl, but there was so much to look forward to and we were so grateful for what we had that we didn't give it much thought.

We were told that she was alert and bright, had a wonderful temperament, smiled easily, ate and slept well, was intensely curious, and absolutely gorgeous. The reason we hadn't been called earlier was that the agency wanted to make sure that she was available for adoption. Her birth father had not signed the papers to release her for adoption, and in New York State at that time, he had six months to come forward.

As a pre-adoption workshop leader, I recently had gone through a painful experience with a couple in the process of adopting a child whose biological mother claimed not to know who the father was. A few weeks after the baby's placement, after the new parents had fallen in love with him and absorbed him into their lives, the police arrived at their house at 2:00 one morning to seize the child. An irate husband and father had gone to the local police station with a court order. He claimed that he had only just learned of the baby's existence and that his parental rights had been violated. The officers seized the baby from the tearful couple.

Fearful of a similar fate, we decided to wait the extra month until the placement would be irreversible, reasoning that the one month would not make that much of a difference in all of our lives and that the peace of mind was worth the trade.

John had a business trip planned for the following week, but arrangements were made for Matt and me to meet Bethany in her foster home and follow up with a few more visits so that she could get to know us and not be too overwhelmed when we brought her home. Since she had spent the first six months in one home we were aware that a sudden transition would be confusing for her, and so we tried to make the move as easy as possible. The best laid plans … a winter flu attacked the foster family and Bethany was the only one who remained healthy. We were told to pick her up after just one brief visit. One day Bethany was living with her foster family, and the next day she was with us.

I cannot describe in words what each of us was feeling; joy and ecstasy are not adequate for the job. But imagine her arrival. We had decorated the house with colorful balloons and cuddly toys. The phone rang constantly with friends and relatives calling for briefings on our progress. Every few minutes Matt would go over to her and touch her and smile at her as we all giggled and laughed, making happy sounds and faces as she stared at us in bewilderment.

Naptime came and we tried to put her in her crib for a rest, but she cried and cried. She was equally unhappy when we picked her up, and she wriggled and squirmed in her discomfort. Because she was obviously exhausted from all the emotional strains of the day, we tried to comfort her. But she would have none of that. Finally, Matt toddled into their room, climbed into the crib, and called for his baby sister who contentedly settled down. The two of them fell asleep together and we were enthralled.

Her sleep was deep and long. Bethany was understandably exhausted from the strangeness of her new home and family, and for the next several weeks she slept almost around the clock. In retrospect, I can see that sleep gave her a chance to retreat from the shock of her new life. It was as if she was saying, "Back off now. Give me time to catch up!" But at the time we were somewhat confused. Nobody had prepared us for this. The social worker, the foster family, and we had assumed that she would sense right away that we loved her, and in return she would love us back, as she slid seamlessly into our family. We didn't even question the past or how we could compensate for the rupture in Bethany's life.

Naively, we had thought that when we adopted Bethany we were removing her from her first home and that our love would help her overcome any problems that this separation created. But in reality, this baby had been abandoned twice. Having spent nine months in utero and six and a half months in a foster home, she now had to acclimate to a third environment. What does a child who has not yet learned to speak understand of this cataclysmic event? Who are these strange people? Where are the people who tended to her? The children who played with her? Why is everything so different today? What happened to yesterday?

For Bethany, it must have been like being tossed into the void with nothing to grab on to. How hard to trust us when she had been snatched so rudely from her familiar home and resettled without any preparation. We had brought her to this place to meet new parents, a new brother, her new grandmother, a dog and two cats. She was going to live in a new world with its unfamiliar sounds and smells. All of the familiar sensual memories that are so crucial to the preverbal child were now replaced by a strange house with its unaccustomed rooms, crib, clothes, toys; the list goes on. And all of this, without language and understanding and without the support of the people she had been so dependent upon who had just disappeared, along with the life that had been her reality until this time.

For our part, we were full of unrealistic expectations, envisioning her immediate responsiveness and affection. As mature adults, we assumed we understood what was happening and that she would embrace our love and quickly forget what had gone before. How naive could we all have been! This same child whom we had been told was so responsive and alert now could not seem to wake up, and when she was awake, she wore this sad expression on her face as if she was mourning the loss of her best friend. Her body was stiff. When we would hold or tickle her or do all the things that parents and their babies do, she would remain rigid and controlled, unable to laugh, as we wanted her to do. Her face was so serious. Was she scared? Was she grieving? Was she depressed? What was she thinking and feeling? Why wouldn't she relax? Now the answers seem so obvious, but at the time, it felt like rejection. I remember thinking then, "I should be cuddling her more." But she wouldn't let me. When I picked her up, she pushed against me as she struggled to get away. Opportunities to hold her were few. Already eating solid food at six months, I could not hold her to feed her a bottle. If she hurt herself and needed consoling, one of us would pick her up to cuddle, but she would quickly recover and push herself and us away. When we should have been holding and rocking her, cooing to her and attempting to soothe her, we let her lead the way and did not force ourselves on her. It was with the best of intentions. We were trying not to threaten her, hoping she would develop trust, but instead we probably were not providing enough opportunities for her to bond. But we wanted those smiles, and so we became more dramatic and effusive trying to elicit her laughter, and we probably frightened her even more.

In a short time, Bethany became a fitful sleeper, kicking and thrashing about until she would eventually fall into a dead sleep with her eyes partially open. Even then she couldn't give herself completely over to sleep. When awake, she would look at us with her serious blue eyes, never smiling, nor showing us the joyful delight which we had been promised was so much a part of her nature. Throughout the rest of her first year, her face displayed a serious world-weary expression, that lacked the captivating smiles that we had eagerly awaited. We had the sense that she was watching and judging us to see what would happen next. It was only Matt who was able to make her smile.

Bethany, smart little child that she was, already controlled our lives. As we watched her every move, we held our breath waiting for her endearing childish laughter that never seemed to come. Perhaps it was then that she learned of the power she had over us. As I write this now, it seems ridiculous. She was only seven months old. How could she have so much control over us so quickly? But she did, and her need for control showed up in other ways as well. Her diapers were remarkably clean. And as she parceled out her laughter, she did the same with her tears, holding them in when tired or frustrated long past when other children would have broken down.

And that is the way it went for that first year. The only one she did not regard with suspicion and apprehension was her brother. The two of them were inseparable. She followed him wherever he went, his constant shadow, and it was for him that she reserved her giggles and laughter. Towards us, she remained tentative and watchful, unable to show us the charm and warmth that endeared her to her foster family.

Though not an expressive child, Bethany was a quick learner. At about eight months, she began walking, and she started talking early, too. But there was already some troublesome behavior. She began biting Matt. Frequently during their play, he would scream with pain when for no apparent reason she would dig her sharp baby teeth into his arm, and nothing I could say would stop her from inflicting this pain on him. When I would take her away for a short while to demonstrate the seriousness of her actions, Matt would beg me to let her come back and play with him. "She didn't mean it," he would explain.

So there were early signs of problems: the biting, the rigidity, the need to control. But we thought we had time as an ally. Time and love would help us build the trust and security that are so essential for a child to thrive.

◆   ◆   ◆

When Sara and John brought Bethany home, she was already seven months old. She had been through what was undoubtedly a difficult in utero experience with a very young birthmother who did not have prenatal care. Bethany had a low birth weight. That is all her adoptive parents knew about her experiences before she was born.

At birth, Bethany had to separate from her biological mother to whom she had been intimately connected for the last forty weeks. With the process of being handed to another mother, she was abruptly forced to give up the world she had become familiar with. "Where did my mother go? What frightening and strange place am I in now?" Even though Bethany could not yet talk, she knew that the whole landscape had changed without warning, and it was beyond her control.

Shortly after birth, Bethany was placed in a foster home with a mother and father and two sisters. Bethany's foster parents told Sara and John that she was bright and responsive, "The best baby they had ever taken care of." Based on this news, they were encouraged. Their hopes were high, as were their expectations for the wonderful life they would all enjoy together.

So they were understandably baffled by Bethany's withdrawn mood and unresponsive face when they brought her home. What they didn't realize at the time was that Bethany was experiencing yet another loss, another sudden separation from a familiar parenting person, a familiar environment. Sara's carefully planned gradual transfer from one home to another had been abruptly cancelled, and that abrupt change was far worse for Bethany than the flu she might have contracted if she had stayed in her foster home, and the original adoption plan had been carried out. Now Bethany was again grieving over a disruption about which she had no control. Suddenly, she was living with strangers. She had to withdraw and shut out the stimulation of the new environment. Even after several weeks in her new home, Bethany could not relax. She was tight, rigid, and preferred not to be held. She couldn't smile, except at Matt, who communicated with her in the language of early childhood.

What could her eager new parents do to help her and themselves in these very difficult circumstances? In hindsight, if they had been better prepared for the realities of Bethany's arrival, they could have adjusted their hopes and expectations that she would be relaxed and happy right away. They could have pared stimulation down to the bare minimum and held her in a quiet place as much as she could allow. They might have felt more comfortable about Bethany's need to withdraw in order to stabilize. They could have been aware of keeping eye contact with her.

Sara stayed home with her children, so she had the opportunity to try to establish herself as the primary figure in her daughter's and son's lives, but she and John might have spent more time encouraging bonding in any and every way that Bethany would allow. In retrospect, they could have chosen to take her home a month earlier-an option they had at the time, but one that they rejected due to the serious legal risks involved.

The major task of the first year of life is for the baby to bond with the mother or primary caregiver. One of the earliest signs of this bonding taking place is smiling in reaction to the human face. By six months of age, infants reserve their smiles for their mothers or very close friends. According to Rene Spitz (1965), a pioneer in infant research and development, infants do not smile at strangers. They are beginning to choose their love objects. The mother has the all-encompassing role in the unfolding of her baby's consciousness and learning processes through the innumerable intimate interactions that occur between them. The baby's smile signals the beginning of trust, the beginning of social relationships.

For Bethany, this vital bonding has clearly been disrupted. She has lost her love object, and she must sustain her deep loss and start over. She simply is not able to smile at Sara and John. They are strangers. She is grieving and depressed. Spitz also helps us understand that at about eight months an infant develops what he calls stranger anxiety. What the baby reacts to in the presence of a stranger is the awareness that this person is not her mother, that her mother has gone away, and that she has been left. This awareness signals that the baby has established a true relationship and her mother has become the focus for her love, distinguished from all others. This bond with the mother is exclusive. Everyone else is a stranger except for her family and close friends with whom the baby feels a sense of familiarity.

Since the age at which stranger anxiety evolves is variable, it is possible that Bethany was already well into this bonding process when she moved into her adoptive home. Sara's descriptions of Bethany's demeanor certainly suggest this to be so. Had Sara and John known this, they would not have been able to prevent Bethany's highly uncomfortable reactions, but they would have better understood what was going on and could have known what not to do as well as how best to soothe their daughter. Had they been better prepared, they might have been less frustrated, less disappointed, and less worried about Bethany's responses. They could have found ways to reassure each other and seek outside support when they felt shut out and ineffective. They would have been better prepared for the parenting job ahead of them. Adoptive parents have little control over the circumstances of adoption: the age of the child, the process of transfer from one parenting person to another, the health of the birthmother, or the inevitable separation of the child from the biological mother who could not parent her. They rarely have complete information about the background of their adopted children that would help them parent. What they do have are opportunities to make choices about the adoption process, to develop reasonable expectations for their parenting role, and to be committed to ongoing learning as their children grow and develop in order to be as effective as possible. They have information about how important it is to nurture themselves while they are engaged in this difficult parenting job.

Babies in agencies, children's homes, or even foster care will probably not have the opportunity for an intimate, interactive, closely attuned experience with a stable mothering person—a necessary experience that stimulates optimal early development. Thus, the chance for early attachment or bonding is reduced or at best altered. This situation is almost always the case in international adoption. So adoptive parents need to be aware of guidelines for attachment (see Appendix A: *OPTIMIZING ATTACHMENT BETWEEN CHILD AND PARENT*) in order to encourage an intimate relationship with their infants.

Recently, Seth Pollack Ph.D. a researcher at the University of Wisconsin reported that, "Children raised in the uncaring environment of some eastern European orphanages ended up with a long-standing deficit in two hormones involved in forming social bonds." The hormones, oxytocin and vasopressin, are small proteins produced by the pituitary gland. Researchers have found that the hormone levels in laboratory monkeys are significantly lower and may affect bonding between mother and child, sexual bonds between males and females, and social interaction. If a correlation can be shown between human beings and the laboratory species it will follow that "early neglect can have a direct effect on neurobiology in ways that later influence emotional behavior."(NY Times Nov. 22, 2005, F5).

Daniel Hughes (1998), a specialist in attachment and adoption, has written extensively about the symptom patterns of poorly attached children and has outlined parenting guidelines for developing attachment. Hughes has carefully broken down a description of attachment patterns by months and has described both optimal and dysfunctional behaviors and attitudes to look for during these stages, from birth to forty-eight months. Parents preparing for adoption will do well to become educated about the attachment information made available through Hughes and others in order to be as well equipped as possible to recognize their baby's level of attachment and work with her on becoming as optimally attached as possible. This will be an ongoing matter of critical interest for adoptive parents throughout the lifetime of their children. In subsequent chapters, we will discuss these guidelines which include the importance of eye contact, touching, hugging, holding, smiling, and rocking.

Dr. Margaret S. Mahler (1975), an eminent child analyst, is credited with groundbreaking work that would eventually illuminate attachment patterns. In the early 1960s, Dr. Mahler was awarded a grant by the National Institute of Mental Health to study the ways in which healthy children attain a sense of identity. She and her staff observed infants and mothers for more than five years in a setting carefully designed for this purpose. Her observations verified the occurrence of four subphases of what she called the separation-individuation process. She details the patterns of mother-child interaction typical of each subphase and the developmental patterns of the child occurring at each subphase. Mahler describes this entire process as the infant's psychological birth.

From the beginning, each child unfolds within the organization of the mother/child unit. The child is usually the far more adaptive of the two and is shaped within the environment of the mother's style and habits. It has been my observation that the opposite is true with adoption; that is, the child is the less adaptive partner.

As the mother and child interact, there are forerunners to the separation-individuation process that occur in the first weeks after birth. The first forerunner phase is the normal "autistic" stage in which the body processes are dominant. The infant is in a half-sleeping, half-waking state, protected from outside stimuli and involved in having basic needs taken care of by another.

The second forerunner phase begins with the second month and marks the phase of symbiosis in which the baby behaves as though she and the mother are a single unit. If this phase is proceeding optimally, the baby experiences a oneness with her highly attuned mother. During symbiosis, there is a sensitivity of the total body surface. Holding and body pressure are important, and eye contact, rocking, talking, and singing to the infant help promote well-being.

Emergence from the symbiotic state is a gradual process and represents a psychic birth experience, a "hatching" process in which the mother is the catalyst, organizer, and activator, according to Mahler. During this period the infant's inner sensations form the core of the self and represent the beginning of what will later be established as a sense of identity.

At about four to five months, the first subphase emerges—"differentiation" and the development of the body image. One to two months later, the first tentative experiments with separation-individuation surface. This is the peak of tactile and visual exploration of the mother's face. Here comes the time of choosing transitional objects, substitutes for the mother's breast or neck which are soft, warm, and full of body odors. In this way, the baby can keep mother with her while not actually holding on to her. During this period, the baby is regularly pulling her body away while being held in order "to get a better look" and to experience feeling her own body as separate from her mother's.

Between seven and ten months "early practicing," Mahler's second subphase, emerges. The baby starts to move out by crawling and pushing away while using her mother as home base to "refuel" through physical contact. She is pushing and pulling away from her mother into the outside world, and she is absorbed in the pleasure of independent functioning. The second part of the second subphase begins from about ten to twelve months and ends around sixteen to eighteen months, so there is an obvious overlap between the first and second year of life. During this subphase, there is upright locomotion, and the baby enjoys what Dr. Phyllis Greenacre (1957) terms a "love affair with the world." At this time, the toddler takes the greatest step toward individuation. She is walking freely and upright which provides her with a totally new and exciting visual perspective of what the world is all about.

Two complementary developments occur in the separation-individuation process. The first, separation, takes place as the child emerges from symbiotic fusion with the mother, leading eventually to individuation. The second, individuation, occurs as the child assumes her own individual characteristics through her experiences and achievements. In normal circumstances, this individuation progresses in a setting of developmental readiness for and pleasure in independent functioning, very much in contrast to the circumstances surrounding traumatic separation.

If we combine Mahler's work with Brazelton and Cramer's contributions to current infant research, we can see how crucial those early months of life are. Even in their first weeks, infants are already taking in cues from their environment. Bethany certainly was exposed to an abrupt, traumatic separation from her foster mother. We can only imagine that her separation from her birthmother was equally as abrupt, representing a sudden loss of all that was familiar in utero.

As an early walker, Bethany separated physically from Sara before bonding could take place. This precocity led to a premature awareness of separateness before Bethany developed any internal resources for coping with this degree of separation. Because she was ready to walk, development demanded that it take place, but psychologically, Bethany was left with no time to bond to her new primary love object before becoming aware of herself as a definitely separate being. If we were able to understand precisely where Bethany was in the separation-individuation process when she suddenly changed parents, we would have the best chance of helping her cope with the adaptations she would have to master. Without that knowledge, Sara and John could parent only by trial and error, combined with their nurturing instincts.

Within this time frame of critical development—birth to three years—certain traumatic occurrences may cause fragmentation, and a child yet unable to talk or communicate may experience panic and trauma over what appears to be a minor incident such as a brief separation or trivial loss (James 1994). These children will be inconsolable until their mother returns. In Bethany's case, it was certainly more than a minor occurrence that affected her during this phase of her development. We can only guess at the level of impact of these disruptions on her sense of stability since it is so difficult to reconstruct a picture of the inner life of the preverbal child. In such situations, the truest form of inference involves observations of the child's body since in a preverbal child motor development expresses the child's internal state. These are the pathways of communication available to the child long before verbal expression takes place.

We know that Bethany was rigid and tightly controlled. She did not want to be touched or held. She screamed loudly and often, and was determined to push her adoptive parents away. From the start, she did not want them to comfort her. Bethany even resorted to biting, and no amount of intervention on Sara's part could deter her daughter from continuing to bite.

If a child has a difficult in utero experience in which her mother is emotionally cut off and not able to participate in a bonding process, or if the child is developing in an environment of drug and alcohol abuse, she will be born with an insufficient ability to connect to another person. She will be developing with a nervous system that is immature, imposing limitations on her ability to function. Possibly, she will even be struggling with a high level of endorphins in her body that will create distinct discomfort. Whether or not any of these conditions apply to Bethany's experience before birth remains unknown.

The earlier a child enters her adoptive home the better. If the adoptive mother takes over immediately after the child is born, the chances of entering into a symbiotic pairing are vastly increased. The baby will still have to adjust to leaving her birthmother and will still be affected by whatever physical and neurological factors occurred in utero, but having to develop with inadequate maternal attention or having to transfer from one mother to another during the separation-individuation phase should be avoided. Lawyers and social workers would be well advised to concentrate their efforts on releasing babies for adoption at birth. If Sara and John had been fortunate enough to adopt Bethany at a younger age, she might have avoided having to detach from her foster mother to reattach to Sara.

Bethany seems to have felt that she needed to accelerate her own development and do everything on her own. She ate solid food early, toilet trained herself early while rarely soiling her diapers, walked and talked early, and refused contact and comfort. It appeared that she was prematurely functioning in areas in which she should not have been able to do so. Later, she refused to cry when hurt, rest when tired, or show frustration when stressed. We will never know with certainty how she was affected by the separations in her first year of life, but her behavior indicates that she did not feel it was safe or acceptable to have age-appropriate needs. This may have led to premature development that could not last as time went on due to inadequate underpinnings. Bethany had to skip part of the bonding period that was already severely compromised in order to move on with what was being demanded developmentally. Emotionally, she was not ready for these steps since she had no reason to trust that a stable mothering person would stay with her and not disappear again.

4

EARLY SIGNS OF TROUBLE: AGES 1 TO 4

"… What a good two-year-old; she hardly needs you!"

Bethany's first birthday arrived and, like most families, we celebrated the occasion with friends and family. Bethany toddled around; she studied the smiling faces of her nearby audience. Set before her was a large ice cream cake, *Happy Birthday Bethany*. She plunged her hands into the cake, gathering as much ice cream as she could and stuffing it into her mouth. We all laughed at our serious little birthday girl with the chocolate smeared face, the adorableness of it all. But the rigidity of her movements and the gravity of her expression were worrisome at such a happy time.

Bethany developed quickly and precociously. At eight months old, she started walking. At a year and a half, she asked questions and spoke in complete sentences. She repeated stories in the very words that she heard only once. She loved to play the piano, picking out little tunes that she quietly hummed as I walked by. She was quite agile and social, and already matched her brother at all the physical activities they played together. What a bright and beautiful child she was. The possibilities for her future seemed infinite!

Life was wonderful! We had everything we always wanted. The children got along well. Bethany's quickness brought comments from friends and adoration from her brother. By this time, Matt was in nursery school a few mornings a week, and on days when he was brought home by another mother, Bethany waited expectantly at the window watching for him and clapping her hands when she saw the car coming down our drive. To the outside world, we were the perfect American family with a lovely home in the suburbs, two beautiful young children who adored each other's company and a house full of assorted pets.

But lurking behind this public perfection was a seriousness that did not seem to dissipate, and from the beginning it worried me. It was close to two years before we heard Bethany laugh with any regularity and saw signs that she was beginning to be at ease. She still didn't want us to hold her for any length of time. She tolerated no quiet time for hugging and rocking or just being close. Bethany had to keep busy and active until she fell asleep exhausted early in the evening. There were, of course, exceptions to this behavior. John could pick her up to dance; the two of them spinning with exhilaration. And on numerous occasions, I remember holding her as we slid down snow covered hills together until she was agile enough to do it on her own. But the calming and peaceful holding of love and affection were too much for her. There could be no quiet reading time. No lying in bed together while we whispered and giggled over shared silliness, the times I cherished from my own childhood.

Whoever heard of a baby who did not want to be held? Don't all small children want to play with their pets, hugging them, dressing them in hats and silly outfits? I decided to teach her how wonderful it is to cuddle and be cuddled. I went to tag sales and bought lots of dolls for her to nurture. I showed her how mommies hold and snuggle with their babies hoping that she would be gentle with the baby dolls that we gave her, but she didn't follow the pattern. Instead, she waited until she was alone and then yanked off an offending body part. The dolls all quickly ended up discarded on the floor, limbs separated from torsos, heads dislocated from trunks. They were not destroyed in anger, were not part of a vengeful rage. They just "broke, Mommy."

One day shortly before Christmas, I went to FAO Schwartz in New York City in search of a doll that would be indestructible. I purchased what the salesman assured me was their strongest model. One guaranteed to outlast its fragile counterparts. Wrong! It, too, soon made its appearance in dolly heaven, a victim of the same force that had destroyed so many other dolls in her room.

Life was filled with contradictions. As reluctant as Bethany was to express her affection to us and the pets and her dolls, adult friends coming to visit were enchanted by her gregarious behavior. Relatives, baby sitters, neighbors remarked on her friendliness with outsiders. She usually outshined her more withdrawn older brother who was reluctant to warm up to strangers. It would be hard for anyone outside the immediate family to fathom what our concerns were, and we couldn't express our fears because our reservations were so vague. We had never been parents before. How were we to know if this was all normal or not?

So, I tried to reason out the cause of our concern about this behavior, in particular, her rigidity and apparent lack of attachment to us. Privately, I blamed myself for not being demonstrative enough. As I was growing up, my own mother had been particularly undemonstrative with her affections. I had vowed not to be that way with my own children, but perhaps, I was unconsciously repeating learned behavior and Bethany was mimicking me.

I worried, too, that I was unintentionally withholding my love from her, subconsciously feeling that she may have usurped the attention that Matt had always had. Each time I engaged in this internal argument trying to find explanations or reason myself out of my fears, I came up against the dolls, and that was frightening. Many little girls love to play with dolls. Why didn't Bethany? Eventually my fruitless reasoning led me to the possibility that there was another cause for this behavior, one that I had no part in creating and couldn't name. I was fighting the demons of self-blame and ignorance.

Pretty soon Bethany's strong will and need for independence began to assert themselves. Matt was being toilet trained so she stopped wearing diapers too. Before we even broached the process of toilet training Bethany, did it herself. One day she was wearing diapers, and the next she was through with them. No accidents. No waiting until the last minute. It was accomplished.

Bethany became very picky about the clothes she would wear. She began choosing her own outfits and dressing herself. If we dressed her and she didn't like what we picked, she would undress as soon as our backs were turned and reappear in another outfit. It was as if Bethany was renouncing childhood and trying to move on with her life as fast as she could by asserting her independence and demonstrating her decision-making skills.

Early on, Bethany learned to disobey the word "No" and finds ways to circumvent it. When we told her that she couldn't have any more cookies or candy she hid them behind a radiator, under her bed or beneath a pile of clothes in her room. Her little collections of sweets, I assumed, were to be eaten at a later time, but the candy was never eaten. Instead, it resurfaced at a later date, green with mold. And she craved sweets, eating handfuls of sugar at a time. With a birth family history of diabetes, this was troublesome for us, but we could not control this behavior either.

Jokingly, I expressed my apprehensions to John about her teenage years. As we projected into the future, we imagined our daughter falling prey to the drug pushers so rampant in our communities. Our fear was that the child who could not "eat just one" and would not accept the word "no" would not develop the self-discipline necessary for later years. And yet, we were very aware of the dangers of the self-fulfilling prophesy.

Sweets were not the only thing that Bethany collected. In little boxes, I found collections of her hair and fingernail clippings. An early nail biter, she was obviously saving these mementos. I recalled conversations in which I told her about her cousins who each have a special collection of tiny treasures—marbles, Matchbox cars, dolls, teacups, but Bethany's collection was unique.

Surprisingly, "no" was a word that Bethany seldom uttered. We expected the "terrible twos" to emerge with that word as its hallmark, but that never happened. Verbally, she was compliant. We took all of this as signs of intelligence, independence, precociousness, alertness, and continued to keep our concerns to ourselves. "What a good two-year-old. She hardly needs you!" outsiders would say.

Meantime, some of her unsettling behaviors were worsening. She threw outrageous temper tantrums when frustrated, screaming hysterically until she wore herself out. We responded by removing her from her surroundings and trying not to place her in a similar situation again. If we attempted to settle her down by holding her during one of these episodes, she squirmed and wiggled until we had to let her go. She had none of the usual pacifiers with which to comfort herself. At an early age, Bethany gave up her bottle, rarely sucked her thumb, rejected her security blankets and had no favorite doll.

But what Bethany did have was the living room couch. She sucked on its arm, drooled over it, spat and rubbed it in with her finger. She acted like a cat marking her territory and it became a family joke.

Bethany could not tolerate being alone. She didn't like to play by herself, look through books, color, or do any of the things that usually engage a young child's attention. She preferred to be active and move around or play with other children. I was constantly arranging play dates for her and when she was three, I signed her up for nursery school. We arrived at a roomful of wailing children being reassured by their mothers. "Don't worry. Mommy will be back." "I can stay if you want me to." "Mommy loves you. Don't cry." "Look at all the friends you'll have." But I needed no such words. Bethany quickly dropped my hand and ran off to take a good look around. I, though somewhat baffled, consoled myself with her early independence and pioneer spirit.

At school, she soon directed her playmates' activities, assigning different roles. There was always the mommy, the daddy, the pets and the baby, Bethany. She climbed into the doll carriage and made baby noises as her friends rocked and cradled her. Calls from other parents who were confused by this behavior put us on alert. What did it mean? Little Bethany, who would not accept nurturing from us and would not nurture her own dolls, was seeking nurturing from her friends.

At about this time, we also began to hear about her biting other children. The teacher called us concerned about the behavior. At home, Bethany had already bitten her brother on occasions when she didn't get her way. Reasoning with her didn't stop the behavior, and separating the two of them wasn't effective either, for it was soon Matt who explained that "She didn't really mean it." Again, we tried to reason with her. "No one will want to play with you if you hurt them, Bethany." But the behavior continued, even escalated.

One time while I was trying to hold her, she turned her head and bit me on the breast. The pain from those sharp little teeth was excruciating. I screamed and tears quickly filled my eyes. Without thinking, almost as a reflex, I smacked her across the mouth. I thought she was startled by my reaction, and so was I. I wondered how Matt and those other children had been able to control their own responses. Anyway, the biting stopped. It was a lesson for me that I should have paid more attention to as it was predictive of later patterns. The talking, the reasoning, the crying of her wounded playmates had no effect on Bethany's behavior; the physical punishment did. At the time, I was filled with remorse.

Prior to adopting Matt, there were many sessions with social workers discussing our attitudes toward discipline and child rearing. Both of us were adamant. We would not hit our children. We believed that if we treated our children with respect, respect for their intelligence and innate morality, they would make the right decisions. Now here we were, the children we dreamed about for years had finally materialized, and one was a biting, tantrum throwing, strong willed creature who responded only to a slap across the face. We didn't read those early signals well and continued doing as we had, naively trusting that these two bright children raised in a respectful and stable home would have the ability and motivation to make intelligent decisions. Even now, when I reread this, I am tempted to say, "Some kids do strange things when they are growing up." Bethany could have been into an exaggerated "terrible twos."

But Matt had not displayed any of these extreme behaviors. That he was a boy accounted for some differences, and birth order could have accounted for others. But where Bethany was cold and aloof, Matt was affectionate and giggly. He was much more responsive to our nurturing. I read to him and held him. We would stare at each other's faces, touching noses and cheeks, singing and making silly faces.

Though equally bright, Matt was slower and more deliberate in all of the developmental benchmarks. He learned to talk one word at a time. His toilet training dragged on for what seemed like forever. He was shy, wary of strangers and tentative in trying new things. But I never worried about him the way I did about Bethany. Matt's temperament was more what we had expected from our child, more childlike I would say. He needed us; whereas she, who was so much more outgoing and less dependent on us for comfort, jarred our sense of balance and astonished outsiders with her precocity. She seemed hell-bent on rushing towards emancipation while it was apparent that Matt wanted to remain a child. Now we know how the story unfolds for Bethany, and I can tell you, her development at this age introduced a range of behaviors that would become more extreme as she got older.

This was the period in our lives when we were very active in an adoption support group. The support group provided opportunities for socializing among the children and, of course, the parents. We were all still elated with the miracle that each child represented, but we would also use the opportunity to discuss, among other things, our concerns about our children's development. I remember one mother who was worried about her child's rigidity of physical movements, her tensed shoulders, her arms bent tightly at the elbow, her awkward walk. She had recently discussed her concerns at an early child development center in her community. Another set of parents was anxious about what they perceived as their child's hyperactive behavior. He was continuously in motion, scooting around the house in his walker or frantically rocking back and forth in a chair. They had gone to a psychologist for a consultation about his behaviors. There was one family whose concern was their son's lethargy and the lack of affect in his facial expressions. It was in these meetings that we first gave public voice to our concerns for Bethany, her lack of affection, her refusal to accept "no" as an answer, her temper tantrums, and her unusually strong will. Like ours, the other parents' misgivings had already been reported to pediatricians who, in most cases, told them not to worry, that everything was probably just fine. The professionals whom we sought assistance from were as uninformed as we were.

Perhaps in any room of fifty young children between the ages of birth and nine years there would be that range of behaviors. Perhaps these oddities were just the extremes of normal behavior. But my reservations were not assuaged by these discussions and so, sometime after Bethany's second birthday, I took advantage of a notice in the newsletter of our support group that offered an opportunity to find out if we really did have a problem. There was a call to participate in a study of bonding patterns between adoptive mothers and their adopted two year olds. I volunteered with Bethany. The study was part of a Ph.D. dissertation and was conducted at Hunter College in New York City. Bethany and I were to be observed behind a one-way mirror as we played, talked and read a story together. The professional conclusion was that everything was as normal as it would have been between a birthmother and her child. I had my doubts. I had been aware that while Bethany had been looking at me at appropriate times during our visit, she was also distracted and discomforted throughout the laboratory study. But this too may have been normal. The report offered no help and I filed it away, disappointed by its lack of insight and information.

As she was moving through nursery school towards kindergarten, we were constantly amazed by all that Bethany could do. She would enjoy dancing and drawing pretty little pictures. She was very agile and delighted in gymnastics where she beamed with exhilaration when she climbed a rope and rang the bell at the top. Bethany loved to sing and softly hummed simple tunes when placed in her car seat as she observed the passing scenery.

At home, Bethany would get on her Big Wheels bike and go speeding down our driveway. I can still see her screeching with delight as she picked up speed, turning just in time to avoid the huge garage doors. She and Matt would rake piles of fall leaves and jump into them with enchanting shrieks of laughter. It was Bethany who would pull a step ladder out so that she could jump from an even greater height. She was our little daredevil, defying the laws of gravity and motion, displaying no fear.

But at night, another Bethany would emerge, one that presaged a more disturbing side. We would awaken in the morning to find her curled up in Matt's bed or on the floor in his room where she had gone after a particularly bad nightmare. Night after night this happened. She never woke us or came to us for comfort. Instead, the next day she would tell us how frightened she had been in the dark. At first, she was satisfied with the nightlights that we placed around the house, but then she told us she needed a fan in her room because the quiet scared her. Even in the winter, its droning sound comforted her as she slept. Later, she requested that her radio be turned on "to keep me company," she explained.

At about this time a change occurred in our household. I went back to work three afternoons a week. We enrolled the children in a local daycare center, and they would go there on those days after school. Matt was now in kindergarten, half day in our community, and Bethany would run to the window at day care to await her big brother's arrival. Then they would play near each other, touching base every short while, checking in. They were still very close.

We were not particularly concerned about leaving them in daycare. It was a nurturing environment where they could play with other children and do creative and physical activities. We viewed it as similar to regularly scheduled play dates. So did they. They loved being there, and it provided social opportunities for the parents as well as the children. It also offered a cohesive community for our family with many friends who watched over the children. Everyone remarked on the closeness between Matt and Bethany, wondering how we had accomplished this.

My childcare leave would soon be drawing to an end, and I knew that I would have to return to work on a full time basis in the near future. I didn't want my return to work to be a cataclysmic event in the children's lives, and this seemed a perfect way to ease them into a new routine. If I knew then what I know now, I might have made a different choice, but being a stay at home mother wasn't a viable option at that time, and it still isn't for many mothers.

When Bethany was somewhat past four, she became noticeably intrigued by matches. "Mommy, matches hot, right mommy?" Thinking that there might have been a discussion at school about the danger of playing with matches, I praised her for her good sense and told her that matches can burn people, and that burns are very painful.

Shortly after that conversation, we headed to the local ball field where John was playing on a baseball team. Sitting in the stands, talking with the other mothers, and watching the game, it took us a while to realize that the children had disappeared. A few of us took off to look for the kids. The children were hidden behind some trees staring in fascination as Bethany attempted to ignite a book of matches.

Here were the beginnings of an emerging pattern. In the interest of showing us how smart and grown up she was, Bethany announced the rationale for not pursuing a variety of activities. But only a short time later, we found that she had been playing with matches, or taking someone else's belongs, or going into a pond, or climbing a tree. Her declaration of the dangers of doing these things should have been read by us as, "I'm going to do this unless you are smart enough to figure that out and stop me!"

The ramifications of these actions were complex, and my mind couldn't take it all in. Think about the matches! Was this a dangerous fascination or just normal childhood curiosity? We flashed back to her dismembered dolls. Were these signs of an unbalanced little girl or were our concerns overblown? Where were the normal controls on her impulses? The ones that even young children develop that say, "I won't do this" or "I can't have this" or "Mommy told me not to do that." I chalked my negative feelings off to overreaction and life went on.

◆   ◆   ◆

From the beginning of Bethany's joining the family at almost seven months, Sara had been concerned and uneasy about her seriousness, tenseness, rejection of affection and physical closeness and what appeared to be a lack of attachment. Even her precocity was a cause of concern. Sara actively looked for help to understand Bethany's lack of comfort and got no significant support or assistance from professionals or the community. Sara and John were on their own in trying to sort out what was happening, without the tools to do so.

Janelle Peterson (1998) has worked with many adopted children and has helped us understand that adoption dynamics present a serious difficulty to the new family's early adjustment. Adoptive parents are hoping their children will make their dreams for a happy family come true, while adoptive children are struggling to survive the upheaval created by one or more traumatic separations in their young lives. The children may be anticipating even more abrupt and unexplainable separations. Understandably, they refuse to form emotional ties which they anticipate will result in the loss of another relationship and bring more emotional pain. While they don't have the words to tell their parents these fears and feelings if they are young, they usually show them by their tension, their serious demeanor, and their general discomfort, that life is not stable.

They try to keep a safe emotional distance in order to prevent further hurt and manage obstacles as best they can. In infants, resistance to cuddling, stiffness, developmental delays, poor eye contact and lack of response to affection are strong signs of a broken bond. These behaviors leave the caregiver bewildered and at a loss as to what to do. Often the parent feels rejected and starts to pull back, especially since she or he was not expecting this response and doesn't understand it. The broken bonds in Bethany's case are the ones she had in utero with her birthmother and with her foster mother. The rejection Sara felt was due to Bethany's inability to reattach to her. But from Bethany's point of view, her reaction was perfectly understandable. How can it be possible for any child who was so dramatically and unexpectedly wrenched away from the only family she knew be expected to give up her old loves and effortlessly bond to a stranger? That would be unnatural and probably impossible.

Usually around ten to fourteen months of age, the child reaches the glorious moment of learning to walk, and a whole new vista of exploration and excitement is spread before her. Many developmentalists feel it is the golden moment of individuation for the human being. According to Louise Kaplan (1978), noted child psychologist and colleague of Mahler, if the child "has been held well enough" she will reach the stage of being able to believe in being held while walking alone. In Mahler's term, this is the practicing phase (ten to eighteen months) where "peek-a-boo" and "catch me" behavior is repeated over and over. Great strides, both figuratively and literally, are being made toward separation. The child's elation is the dominant mood because of her sense of accomplishment.

In Bethany's development, she started to walk early before she could have possibly believed in a home base in the form of her mother, the center for attachment. Often the child in the practicing phase is so intent on her own explorations she seems to have forgotten her mother. Still, every so often, the child returns to her parent, needing to touch base, needing her physical presence. The tired infant is rejuvenated by these contacts. Her reconnection with her mother provides the opportunity for refueling, and she is again ready to go explore. In order to retain her emotional balance, a precocious walker especially needs a parent's constant availability. If a parent is away or otherwise occupied, the baby will have to work hard not to fall apart. But, according to Sara's description, Bethany was already insistent on doing everything herself and not availing herself of her adoptive mother's comfort and assistance because she did not bond with Sara. Bethany insisted on going it alone, even though Sara was available to her.

At eighteen months, a huge developmental transformation occurs in a toddler's life, one that has a number of critical elements. She has developed a thinking mind that can now use abstractions in the form of symbols, images, and concepts. As a result of the mind's capacity to create and deal with these abstractions, a more mature ability for language develops, and the baby starts to use words to express more complex ideas. As the toddler's mind becomes involved with ever more intricate processes, the emergence of emotions marks another critical development. The child can pretend one thing is another thing. She can communicate. She can retain several images at once. Her parent can be seen as one image, herself as another, and this knowledge of their separateness scares her and creates a crisis. As she becomes more aware of her surroundings and her separateness, she loses her belief that she can conquer the world and feels her own vulnerability. She also loses that sense of delight about walking and exploring, her feelings turning to sadness. In Mahler's terms, she is going through a second birth, a new beginning. Kaplan calls this stage of development the cycle of ecstasy and despair that she believes operates for all of us throughout the rest of our lives.

From ages one to three, brain development is critical. During the first three years, the experiences of life organize the brain and set the stage for future functioning. If interaction and attention from a parent are less than "good enough," certain brain capacities, while not totally lost, are very difficult to stimulate into development at a later stage. The separation-individuation process described in Mahler's work shapes the human being. If that goes wrong, a person will have trouble loving, feeling and being a mature adult. Mahler describes the third phase, which occurs between fifteen to twenty-four months as a highly sensitive and critical phase and calls it the "rapprochement crisis." Since the need for closeness has been held in abeyance during the practicing phase, once there is an awareness of separation, the toddler has a great need to share everything with her parent and be loved by him or her. There is a pattern of shadowing and darting away. There is a fear of loss of mother's love, and the parent's sensitivity to the toddler's needs in this stage will make a great deal of difference in her future relationships.

With the emergence of what Kaplan calls the "thinking baby" around eighteen months, the explosive temper tantrums and unpredictable moods begin. Typically, tantrums are not to be feared and squashed. They can be understood as discharging tension and bringing inner peace. The tantrums arise from the strain of the second birth. The child's job is to find the right distance from her mother in order to maintain both a sense of oneness and of separateness. This is a hard job, one that will go on being developed and refined throughout life.

By the end of the second year, if things have gone well, the process has been successful in building a reliable image of the mother which the toddler carries inside herself as she moves out into the world. The development of language helps this process, and the child learns to say and understand the word "I."

Spitz helps us understand another critical aspect of development during this time frame of one to three years by describing the importance of the toddler's learning the words and gestures to indicate "no." "No" helps the child establish the proper distance and boundaries. It is the first sign of an abstract concept. "No" states the separateness between child and adult and indicates a new level of autonomy. The use of "no" against the loved person puts words in place of attack. Action has been replaced by communication, and Spitz believes that this transition is what started human life on the road to being civilized.

Bethany had trouble with the concept of "no" when used by her parents and rarely used the word herself to assert her separateness. Perhaps she couldn't do so, since her precocious development did not allow her the opportunity to move through the necessary stages toward separation at a comfortable pace. She became seemingly separate without the underpinnings of practicing separation that she needed.

Many children at age two will also start toilet training. At this time, the two-year-old is thinking in black and white—all good or all bad. Each time the child is less than perfect, she will be confused and struggle to understand the reliability of herself. Understandably, toilet training can become problematic if accidents are viewed as being bad, or are used as a backdrop for struggles for control. Control was very important for Bethany as it is for many other adopted children. In fact, to be in control of every situation in order not to be caught off guard is often a life and death issue. Bethany exercised such rigid control that she toilet trained herself with no interaction between herself and the adults in her life.

Most two-year-olds want to hold onto their own body products. They are not yet clear that their bodies belong to them. As they begin to realize through separation experiences that their bodies do indeed belong to them, there is often a realization of the ability to stand on their own, to be separate, safe, and supported. At this age, a child is not sure which body parts fall off and which don't. Awareness of anatomical differences is confusing and, for a girl, sometimes frightening and a source of anger. Perhaps Bethany's insistence on dismembering all of her dolls was an effort to solve the puzzle of body parts, and not a hostile act, as Sara feared. Her habit of saving pieces of her fingernails and bits of hair may have had the same source: her concern over losing body parts.

At two and three, the toddler's working conscience has not yet developed. It will start to emerge at five or six and not be stable until nine or ten years old. First, impulses have to be in place, and through the third year, impulses require control from the outside. A child between the ages of one and three is trying hard to manage tensions and impulses, and as a result, may have fears that seem unusual to the observer. For instance, some children are afraid of being flushed down the toilet. Some develop fears of a certain picture or wallpaper pattern because of what they see in it. It reminds them of something that is scary. These fears are perfectly normal and not anything to worry about; although, it is helpful if the child can talk to someone about them.

Optimally, by age three, the child will have some control over her impulses and will have an awareness of being herself and separate from all others. She has the task of trying to hold onto the feeling of reliability about herself, having a perception of a good self and having a good "inner mother" that she carries with her. She must be able to do all of this in order to have a sense of well-being. She'll eventually learn she doesn't have to be perfect—nor does her parent. She'll learn to accept that she feels love and hate just as we all do and that the experience of being human with all its imperfections is good enough. Peterson very poetically tells us that if the child can be a part of the earth with feet of clay and retain her dreams of glory and ability for illusion, she will have achieved optimally in the first three years of life. Her inner self will be fixed and permanent, reliable, no matter where she goes even though this reliability will be tested over and over when she is operating out of her comfort zone or over-stressed. She will have achieved the state of constancy as described by Mahler. She is now a distinct individual.

As the child moves into age four, there is an expansiveness, a creativity and a youthful ability for fun, silliness, and fantasy which are very much in evidence. One of the most important guidelines at this time is to enjoy this age and not start the child in kindergarten too soon. Material from the Gesell Institute Child Study strongly suggests placing a child in school according to her behavioral age rather than her chronological age, giving special attention to children born in September or after.

In the developmental picture for an adopted child, there are extra stresses during this time frame of one through four. Often the baby feels she cannot count on anyone and has to be self-sufficient since her parent may disappear at any time. Nancy Verrier, in her book *Primal Wound* (1999, 31), tells us about a memory one of her adopted patients describes: "It was as if I figuratively sat up in my crib and said to myself, 'I can't trust anyone. I will have to take care of myself.'"

A child's development is altered by separation from the birthmother. It feels to the child as though the world is hostile and distrustful. After that loss, a child put into the consistent care of another mother figure will most likely be aloof and distant for some time. Bethany went through this traumatic separation from a mother twice. For some children, there are more than two separations, even further weakening the ability for attachment.

Verrier describes the primal experience for the adopted child to be abandonment; the core issues are loss and fear of further abandonment. From Verrier's experience working with a number of adopted individuals, she describes a body of shared feelings and ideas about the world. Often there are difficulties in relationships, a fear of rejection, which starts here: "After all, a mother wouldn't give up a good baby; therefore, I must have been a bad boy." "If my mother couldn't love me, who can?" There is shame for being a bad baby, shame for being who one is. There is a feeling of something missing—of not being whole. There is also the fear that the adoptive parents would have loved a biological child more.

The permanency of relationships is often threatened by this lack of trust with its discomfort with closeness and intimacy, a need for distancing and a need to be perfect. The adopted child or adult adoptee may feel alienated from both the adoptive parents and the fantasized birth parents. In spite of these feelings, there is reason to believe in the ability to overcome the effects of early trauma.

These children and adults need the opportunity to acknowledge their losses and have permission to mourn. If this does not take place, the mourning will be stored psychologically and the result will be depression and unresolved grief that will show itself in various ways. In Bethany's case, it showed in her inability to smile or laugh, in her inability to sleep in a relaxed manner, in her inability to trust and attach, and accept help from others when needed.

Even what looks like a healthy childhood adjustment, such as in Matt's case, can be the development of a false self in an effort to avoid further abandonment. When this happens, the main intent is to keep intact the wall that has been built to keep others at a safe emotional distance, while doing things "right" so that others will find no good cause for throwing him away—the need to be perfect. The cost in personal energy is enormous when this happens, and there may be very little energy left over for moving on with life in a productive way.

With a few notable exceptions most professionals do not understand that adopted children are grieving, nor has it been well addressed in the literature. Lois Melina, in her book *Making Sense of Adoption* (1984), has provided guidelines for parents about how to help their adopted children grieve and be more comfortable with the inevitability of this process. Jeff LaCure, a professional in the field of adoption and an adoptee himself, has developed this theme in his adoption workshops. He describes, in depth, the reactions and feelings of adult adoptees to this profound loss and the sadness of "not being able to say goodbye."

Those who are adopted need to learn to trust the fact that, indeed, they are good people caught in a complicated set of circumstances that asked far more of them developmentally than was asked of children who did not have to change parents at critical stages of growth. That fact, which often cannot be fully understood until adulthood, could possibly allow for some true understanding of the worth and dignity of the person and the difficulty of the life experiences they have undergone.

All experiences with human love throughout life will involve the longing to restore a sense of oneness and the desire to reconnect with a parent's unconditional love while feeling just as deeply a need to remain separate as an individual. The adopted child has the extra task of coming to terms with the untimely and unexplained separation from a mother to whom she was intimately connected, but who will possibly never be seen or known. This concept needs to be fully understood by everyone participating in the adoption process if a stable sense of self is to be achieved.

5

ENTERING THE WORLD: THE EARLY SCHOOL YEARS

"Mommy, how will my birthmother know that Matt and I are all right?"

Kindergarten came for Bethany, and she was so excited. She would have lots of new friends, she would be with her brother, and she would be very smart. Unlike many mothers I knew, the kindergarten screening process was not something that concerned me. I was confident that Bethany was bright and that she had good social skills. The troubling behaviors we had seen had been confined to home, so we anticipated an easy school adjustment.

Our friends had other experiences though. Frequently, their children had learning problems that presented themselves in a variety of ways and became more apparent as the time got closer to begin school. Screening for learning disabilities at this time would provide a setting where their children would begin to feel their differences and what might be the first major assault on their self-esteem. The parents approached the beginning of school with nervous anxiety about their children's adjustment and acceptance in the competitive educational system.

Even we had felt some concern when Matt approached kindergarten. He was by nature very shy, and it took him a long while to warm up to strangers. He would be perfectly content to play by himself, making fanciful and intricate constructions with his Legos, browsing through books, playing with dinosaurs, or digging in the sandbox or snow. But try to engage him in conversation, and he would respond with one-word answers that were laboriously doled out. As his screening approached, we were concerned that a learning problem, perhaps a language disorder, might be identified, but surprisingly, this didn't happen. For Bethany, though, we had no such worries and, as predicted, kindergarten went smoothly. She continued to make friends, quickly picked up the rudiments of reading and writing, and was clever with arithmetic and story telling. She appeared to be a star, succeeding in every way that a parent would want for their young child. We hoped it was a portent for successful schooling and a love of learning.

It was at about this time that I returned to work full time as an English teacher. As I had to leave the house at 6:30 in the morning John would get the kids dressed and fed and then drop them off at school, the first ones there in the morning. They didn't like "being first," so sometimes to sweeten the routine, they would have breakfast out before going to school. They looked forward to the treat and to the time spent together. Within a few minutes of their arrival at school, other youngsters would join them, and they all waited together for the building to open officially. Soon there was a small group of children whose parents both worked, and they would all play in the school gym that had been opened to accommodate them.

On most days I was home by 4:30 PM and would immediately pick the kids up at day care or at a friend's or after school program, but it was a long day for all of us. Matt and Bethany were both involved in after school activities. In varying seasons, soccer, softball, baseball, music, art, dance, and gymnastics crowded their days. Now I think, "What were we crazy?" We were so afraid our children would be left behind that we were manic in providing them with the enrichment we believed was crucial to their success in life. Often Bethany would tell me of her dream. "I dreamt that you were home all day and met me at the door with a plate of cookies that you baked just for me." Her stated desire for a stay at home mother troubled me too, but there was nothing I could do about that. By now we needed the income, and I enjoyed the stimulation of my job.

I made some attempts to find work closer to home, but gave up the search as it became apparent that teachers with twenty years of experience were not going to be hired in budget conscious school districts. And though she repeated the dream to me her behavior belied the wish. She seemed perfectly content at school and at daycare. When holidays arrived providing opportunities to be together she would want to be with her friends, not with me. Matt didn't seem at all concerned about my working and its impact on his life. Feature articles at the time encouraged me with the promise of independent children whose lives were enriched by their varied activities. So I went to work everyday and consoled myself with the knowledge that many mothers worked outside of the home, and their children were perfectly fine.

At home it was always hectic. After picking up the kids, there was shopping, cooking, homework, planning for the next day, cleaning up from dinner, reading, and then bed. We were on this tight schedule where everything had to be squeezed into our routine. I came home with mounds of papers to correct, books to read and lessons to plan. Again, there was little time left for just being together for comfort and fun.

But we were so invested in this life style that I completely missed the indications that, in this case, Bethany might have done better with less activity and more of me.

Is this twenty-twenty hindsight? Over analysis? Simplistic thinking? Unresolved guilt? At this point, I'm not really sure. Soon things started to disappear. I would be unable to find a favorite pin or sweater. Maybe I misplaced it or left it at a friend's. John too would notice clothes were missing—a T-shirt or baseball cap. But we were so busy in our lives that we attributed many of these disappearances to absent-mindedness. Then a pretty hand forged key from an antique desk disappeared. We blamed that on a visiting school friend. When several kitchen spoons vanished we cited hasty kitchen clean-ups as the cause. We lived with these riddles for quite a while.

Two ideas placed together in a narrative make connections seem so obvious, but at the time this was happening, nothing was obvious. It was not, "Well, you went to work, and Bethany felt abandoned so she stole to get your attention." Would that it was so simple! We had not as yet linked Bethany to the missing items. On any given day she was getting commendations in school, writing poetry, sewing little quilts, painting, playing the flute. She was bright and charming and everyone was drawn to her disarming manner and expressive big eyes. She had many friends; she was healthy and active. When I picked her up at day care she would fuss because she wanted to stay with her friends. She was a normal little girl with a lot of energy. Sometimes she complained of nightmares and sometimes she showed a strong temper but none of these behaviors taken by itself was that unusual. In fact, to an outsider she looked close to perfect.

Bethany's entry into first grade marked her developing exposure to the outside world and to an independent social life. She came home one day very upset because in school the talk had been about the death of Lisa Steinberg, a child from New York City, who had been illegally taken by a lawyer and raised by his wife and himself as their adopted child. Steinberg had been a drug abuser and had beaten Lisa to death. "Mommy, how will my birthmother know that Matt and I are all right?" she asked.

At dinner we discussed how we could reassure their birthmother about their well being. Although Matt didn't express his concern, being always the more reticent with expressing his feelings, we were sure he was thinking about it too. Bethany articulated her concerns openly. The outcome of our dinner time talks was that we all decided to write a letter to their mother to tell her how they were, what they were doing and to enclose their school pictures. We sent this to the adoption agency to hold in case their worried birthmother contacted them. Whenever there was an adoption related event or question we used it as an opportunity to discuss the subject with them in an effort to make them comfortable with their identity.

It was in first grade when the facade in school began to show tiny cracks. We had, as I mentioned earlier, a concern about Bethany's consumption of sweets because of the family history of diabetes. We tried to limit her sugar intake, so on most days her school snack consisted of fruit or some other healthy treat. Perhaps one day a week I would pack cookies, but I did not keep them around the house. Experience had shown me that if they were readily available Bethany would devour the entire bag as soon as it had been unpacked. If I attempted to hide them she would scour the house until she uncovered my hiding places. She could show no restraint.

In first grade, her teacher called to tell us that Bethany was taking her classmates' sweets during lunch and suggested we not deprive her of them. Of course, we had not deprived her; we only tried to limit her consumption. In order to defend herself, Bethany told her teacher that I would not allow her to eat sweets because they were not good for her.

Snacks were not the only things she was stealing. The concerned teacher reported the "borrowing" of crayons, glitter, markers, all the things that Bethany had in abundance at home but had told the teacher that her mother would not buy for her. Now we became aware of a troubling new fact about our daughter. Bethany had no qualms about lying to cover up her misbehavior, and unsuspecting adults wanted so much to believe her.

We began to connect the dots from the mysterious disappearances at home to the stealing in school and, of course, we speculated about causes and explanations. We questioned our own behaviors. It was already so confusing. Why did she want my clothes or her father's? Why did she take a pin when she never even seemed interested in it when I wore it? If she took these things where were they? Why couldn't she follow our suggestion and just ask for what she wanted? Was she also taking things at her friends' homes?

Questions and more questions, but no answers. Was this behavior the same as what we had seen when she had ignored the word "no" at an earlier age or her refusal to accept limits on her food cravings? Here was another sign that this child could never have enough. Enough what? Sweets? Crayons? Attention? Love? She seemed to be trying to fill a void inside of herself. We sensed this overpowering need, but initially couldn't put it into words. She did not seem to be developing any self-discipline, and this concerned us.

In our own lives we had often remarked that it was self-discipline that allowed people to accomplish their goals and that its absence limited the scope of a person's life. Bethany could not accept boundaries from us. How would she ever be able to set her own? Her misdeeds seemed to fall into two categories: inappropriate but unconscious behaviors such as the dismembering of the dolls, and purposeful and willful misbehaviors exemplified by the lying, hoarding of food and taking from others. Even today, I have a hard time using the word "stealing," but that is really what this six-year-old was doing. It seemed that as Bethany was growing, so was our list of concerns.

We wrestled with how to handle the problem. Reasoning and scolding her seemed to be ineffectual. Sending her to her room was inappropriate. Punishing her with separation from her friends was likely to backfire and corporal punishment was out of the question.

Growing increasingly concerned about what was happening and where it was heading, we took Bethany to see the first child psychologist. We had heard Dr. Son speak at a PTA meeting. She was introduced as someone who was familiar with children's school and social issues and it seemed like a logical place to start.

Dr. Son appeared to be sensitive to children's feelings and to be knowledgeable about the developmental needs of elementary age children. She touched briefly on the subject of adoption which was fine with us. At the time, we did not think too much should be made of this or that it was necessarily related. Our feeling was that if our children did have problems, it would be too easy to place the blame on their adoption, obscuring other causes. Maybe she would provide the advice we needed. When we made our first appointment, we were hopeful that she could explain what was happening with Bethany.

At the consultation, we described our concerns. Bethany seemed to be overly controlling and so needy for things. Anything that she fancied she helped herself to, and she threw temper tantrums or lied if she didn't get her way. Bethany knew no limits and placed few controls on her appetites. There was never enough of anything to satisfy her. When she was frustrated because things didn't go her way or she didn't get what she wanted, she would often destroy her toys and clothing. But, as we saw it, even more serious was our concern that Bethany didn't seem to have any trust. She couldn't trust us to tell us what was happening in her life or what she was feeling; she couldn't trust herself to try new things and to challenge her abilities. We described a smart and talented child who we were afraid would not thrive in the world. She would be limited by her insecurities and fears, and we did not know how to help her.

Dr. Son met with Bethany for several sessions and then arranged to see all of us for several more. She was charmed by Bethany's easy-going banter and pronounced her perfectly fine. There was no need for alarm. How reassuring to hear that from an expert! We breathed a sigh of relief and tried to put our worries aside.

In fact, life with Bethany did improve for a time. The following year she was chosen along with several other children to be profiled in a book about adoption. Bethany, now eight, talked easily about the subject, her thoughts about her birth family, and her hopes for the future. Towards the end of the interview, she talked about her dream of being a dancer, "I don't take lessons yet, but at home, I create my own movements and I'm good. That makes me happy, but not as happy as I feel being adopted and having my mom and dad. I'm most happy for that!" We could easily hear the self-confidence and exuberance in her words. Adoption didn't seem to be a problem for her. The author, an experienced children's writer who had interviewed hundreds of youngsters for a variety of books, told me how impressed she was with Bethany's maturity and stability. Without sharing our fears, we were again reassured by the words of an "expert."

In the meantime, Bethany continued to do well in school. She enjoyed gymnastics, soccer and softball, joined the Brownies, showed some talent in art and had been labeled a gifted math student. Two piano teachers saw early promise in her abilities, and she played the violin and sang in the school chorus. Although she had many talents, Bethany wouldn't put any effort into developing them. She refused to practice on the violin or piano and would not learn to read the notes. For a while, she got along by memorizing the music until the pieces became too complex. Her teachers became frustrated by her casual attitude, and she grew unhappy with their lack of adoration, so she gave up her music lessons.

At school, she refused to participate in the gifted and talented program, saying she needed more free time. We were disappointed. After all, we knew how bright she was and wanted her to have the intellectual challenges that such programs would provide. We also wanted Bethany to stay connected to friends who would stimulate her intellect and provide a social structure for her outside our family. But it was ultimately her choice. We would not force Bethany to do what she was obviously so opposed to. Perhaps, she was right and did need time to herself, time to be private and away from the competitive academic environment.

We had thought our life together was getting better, but we were only in the lull before another storm. Her petty thievery began to escalate. Where she had once taken crayons and markers from her classmates and an occasional item from home, she now took clothing, jewelry and money on a regular basis from us. John noticed twenty dollars missing from his wallet, then a favorite sweatshirt. Where the loot disappeared to, we never discovered.

Sadly, we confronted her, but she denied everything. Our house, surrounded by acres of undeveloped woods, provided many hiding places. When a sweater of Matt's disappeared and she denied taking it, she was not even chagrined when her school photo showed her wearing it. We repeated what we had been telling her from early on, "Bethany, if you want to borrow something, just ask. Then we can keep track of it. But if you take someone else's things without permission that's stealing, and your friends won't trust you anymore and neither will your family." Here were the echoes of the message we had delivered when she was biting her friends in nursery school.

As Bethany prepared to leave elementary school, we took stock of our little girl. She was beautiful and bright. She could be charming and articulate. People were drawn to her, and she had the capacity to achieve in so many ways. In school, her marks were good and we heard no complaints about her behavior or social problems. Her final report card in elementary school read—"Bethany has had an excellent year. She is a strong student and a super young lady. Bethany is very bright. She is capable of many great things. She needs to learn how to balance social experiences with schoolwork. It has been a pleasure working with Bethany this year!"

But at home we saw another side. She stole. She lied. She needed immediate gratification for all of her desires. She disobeyed and could not control her appetites. She had developed no self-discipline and she refused to challenge herself in any intellectual way. We were very concerned about where all of this might be heading.

◆   ◆   ◆

In most families, the first formal opportunity for assessing how their young child is doing compared to her peers is the screening process for kindergarten. In Bethany's case, there were no questions raised at this point in her development, even though at home her parents were uneasy about a number of behaviors she displayed. For many children at age five, early signs of learning problems, or physical differences, will be noted by professionals in the schools. Perhaps there is a language development issue, an awkwardness of gait or poor coordination, eye problems or a lack of reading readiness; all of which can complicate school adjustment. Families hearing these assessments often find out that their children will be placed in a special class, referred for speech and language therapy, or given an extra service, such as preparation for reading.

At times, this service or placement will be temporary, and the child will quickly "catch up" to her peers and continue on in the school in the usual expected fashion. For other children, this beginning will characterize what will be a long road of frustration, pain and often shame, as they watch their classmates move on with ease while they struggle to keep up. Very often they begin to feel like second class citizens in school as they are singled out for services for a variety of reasons. Some will be accelerated due to an assessment that they are gifted and should take on higher level functioning as happened with Bethany. For others, there will be developmental delays and learning and coordination problems, and they will be referred for remedial services.

There are also those children whose functioning appears to be expectable and average, but who don't like school and feel unhappy in that environment. This situation raises a red flag that something is not as it should be, and often a referral for psychoeducational testing is made to determine if there are subtle inconsistencies in functioning that are making school life difficult for this particular child. While there will be children coming to school everyday hungry, dirty, tired, or stressed by a chaotic home life, there are also children coming to school who are highly anxious or depressed or who appear to their classmates to be a little "odd" for other reasons. These youngsters too will be referred for additional evaluation. In fact, in these early years, school becomes a laboratory for diagnosing and assessing where each child fits in the network of people with whom he will be spending a large amount of time for the next twelve years.

Very early diagnosis holds the best promise for the most successful outcome for each individual child. For the large percentage of children in the midrange, life will hold the usual strains and challenges of growth and development. For the others, those challenges will exist as well as additional ones imposed by the existence of the difficult or superior functioning that have been highlighted during the assessment process.

In the last half of the twentieth century, we have become much more sophisticated about the growth and development process of the human being. As relevant information has reached the general public, earlier intervention has begun. With the emergence of early childhood centers for young children and increasing numbers of day care facilities that serve children from families in which both parents work, there is a better chance that a child with a difference that could become an obstacle to learning is going to be observed and singled out for help. For children with clear-cut differences or issues, there is often a referral for treatment or testing of one kind or another. With these professionals and service programs in place, it is still the parents who bear the ultimate responsibility for seeing that their children get the attention they need at this stage of development, paving the way for following stages.

Yet, there are many children who do not stand out as having unusual needs until they reach kindergarten age, and by second or third grade learning disabilities can create major problems in the classroom. Children who can't keep up with their classmates in reading will often start the process of lying or avoidance to hide this shortcoming. Depression follows close behind, as the child feels bewildered and ashamed that he isn't as capable as his classmates. Often children who were well liked and sought after by friends for play dates and sleepovers start to find themselves left out and a circular process of failure and withdrawal or acting out begins as the child attempts to avoid further defeat and pain. While this process is certainly not confined to adopted children, the percentage of adopted children with these patterns is very high.

Fortunately, none of these circumstances emerged at this time for Bethany. She seemed to be one of those endowed children who have it all—a bright mind, the ability to be successful socially, apparent physical heath, and appealing looks.

Because children at this age lack stable learning and behavior patterns there might be an early assessment of a particular need. A short time later, this same child will be pronounced fine by her school system. But when parents continue, at this point, to see their child not keeping up, or not thriving emotionally, there is sometimes a move to seek help privately, through assessment and treatment. At times, there is a choice made to transfer a child to a private school where there will be fewer children and more opportunity to give attention to the specific issues at hand. For many children, these measures will be sufficient, and the road to feeling competent and successful will be smoothed out. For others, the search for the right setting, the right treatment, the appropriate set of circumstances to bring success will be ongoing, and parents will be struggling every step of the way to find the mix of ingredients that will help their child grow and feel she belongs.

An informal survey of therapists, wilderness programs, emotional growth schools, and mental health centers indicates an unusually high percentage of adopted children with learning and behavior problems. In fact, David Brodzinsky in his book *Being Adopted: The Lifelong Search For Self* (1993) writes, "For children between six and eighteen, though, a number of studies have shown that being adopted is a risk factor for having certain psychological problems, especially low self-esteem, academic problems, and a range of rebellious activities known as 'acting out' behaviors: aggression, stealing, lying, hyperactivity, oppositional behavior, and running away." (Brodzinsky 1993, 9). Many of these youngsters struggle with ADD or other genetic conditions and are diagnosed with a need for medication in order to function well in school. Many have social problems as well. They find it hard to make and keep friends or to learn how to behave appropriately in a circumscribed social setting. Therapists are now working with social groups in an effort to teach children how to be with their peers. Here they are taught how to be cooperative and productive as they interact, a process that some children find impossible to learn on their own.

For Bethany, the problems that started to surface at this time had to do with taking things from others: food, crayons, glitter, markers, clothing and then lying to cover up her actions. Sara felt Bethany was never satisfied, never had enough and did not seem to be developing any self-discipline or any ability to hear the word "no," indicating an inability or unwillingness to accept boundaries.

As Sara also pointed out with Bethany, even bright children sometimes have the puzzling quality of not seeming to value their talents and have no innate interest in pursuing learning of any kind. Bethany did not want to practice her music, nor did she want to be in the gifted and talented program for which she was recommended. Often with children with attachment problems, there is an inability to pursue learning or relationships, to follow through on any level or to strive for excellence.

For the parent attempting to find services and supports for their children during these early school years, there is often considerable frustration and feelings of failure due to the difficulty of finding professionals who can understand what is going on with their children. As Sara pointed out in her experience with Dr. Son, the therapist was misled by Bethany's charm and obvious brightness and judged her to be doing fine and developing normally, but this was very far from the truth. Had Dr. Son taken a careful history, had she listened closely to John and Sara's reporting of events at home and their obvious anxiety about Bethany's development, had she probed beneath the surface of Bethany's well constructed facade, she might have come to a different conclusion. But it is equally true that she might not, under any circumstances, have seen what she needed to see at this stage in Bethany's development. It should be well understood that a thorough assessment cannot take place in one session. A true understanding of a child's emotional underpinnings can take a year—often more time than insurance coverage will allow, suggesting a financial responsibility for the family.

Parents of adopted children need to look carefully for therapists and other professionals who know a great deal about the dynamics of adoption as well as about the specific dynamics of the particular child with whom they are meeting. They may need to seek a second opinion if they do not feel the first therapist made an accurate assessment of their child, an option that Sara and John might have taken. Furthermore, if problems persist, they must reject the somewhat easy answers that their fears are unfounded or that they are to blame for any difficulties.

Some will accuse adoptive parents of being overly sensitive to normal acting out behaviors: "Oh, you are just exaggerating. All kids go through these stages. She'll grow out of it;" or living out a self-fulfilling prophecy—"If you keep looking for these problems, you'll find them." Adoptive parents should listen to their own inner voices and tune into their intuition in spite of the feedback of professionals or friends who often say, "Don't make too much of the fact that she is adopted." The difficulty, of course, is in selecting that one piece of information that will add to the parents' understanding of the problem and enhance their ability to deal effectively with it. Helpful ideas can come from a variety of sources and should never be discouraged. Indeed, every effort to help an adopted child become grounded before the turmoil of adolescence hits, is effort that is well placed even if the outcome does not provide immediate answers.

It would be helpful, for adoptive parents in particular, to understand the changes in psychological and educational thinking as they have evolved. Even twenty-five years ago, many educators and therapists were advocating that a child could not be appropriately assessed until age six. There were not yet tools developed for that process, and it was widely accepted that until that age, a child was in a state of flux, of expectable disequilibrium. Some private schools even refused to accept boys into first grade until age seven, since it was understood that boys develop at a slower rate and would not be developmentally ready until then for the tasks demanded of them. Contrast that idea with today's push to start children learning and achieving specific academic goals at ever earlier ages.

As an aid in understanding the course of development from birth until age six, we turn to Anna Freud's book *Normality and Pathology of Childhood: Assessments of Development* (1965) in which she shares with us her concept of developmental lines and how the lines are assessed in each child. For instance, an example of a developmental line would be the movement from dependency to emotional self-reliance and, finally, mature relationships and would encompass all of the steps leading to this achievement. Other lines lead from suckling to self-determination in eating, from wetting and soiling to bladder and bowel control, from irresponsibility to responsibility in body management, from egocentricity to companionship, from the body to the toy and from play to work. In the latter line, she has described that engagement in the play activity itself gives way increasingly to the pleasure of the outcome of the activity, that is, a pleasure in task completion and in problem solving. Some authorities judge this development to be an indispensable ingredient for successful school performance.

Anna Freud tells us that growth along developmental lines will be irregular in many children. Moderate disharmony is not a problem as it produces the many variations of normality that we experience in every day life. But if these lines are too divergent or not sufficiently even in growth by age six, closer examination of the reasons for the unevenness is called for. If a harmonious personality is to eventually emerge an intervention may be necessary.

Sara and John were right to be concerned about Bethany's lack of interest in excelling in school when she was obviously so capable of high achievement. Bethany had moved easily along most of the developmental lines, but here she appears to have hit a roadblock. Bethany was not able to develop pleasure in task completion and seemed to have little or no interest in her own achievements. She definitely was not proceeding along developmental lines in this area.

Any assessment then of the child should be carried out not on the basis of chronological age, but in terms of the psychological differences between mature and immature, and with an eye to Anna Freud's lines of development. Foremost is the question of whether the child is ready to leave home, give up closeness to her primary caregiver and enter group life without experiencing distress of undue proportion. If a child is entering kindergarten, or even nursery school, and is not yet prepared for separation from home and her primary caregiver, the stage is not age adequate and is not appropriate for her as yet.

I am reminded of Jamie whose parents came to me with various concerns when he entered kindergarten. He had come to his family at the age of one year after having been abandoned as an infant and then raised in a children's home in Latin America. Jamie developed well, was observably bright and seemingly well attached to his family. However, at age five, as he entered half-day kindergarten followed by a half-day in a private enrichment program, he developed strong separation issues. He refused to get off the bus in the mornings, was visibly shaken by the experience of going into the school and cried and trembled for the first few minutes in the building. This behavior went on for a number of weeks.

The experience of going to the enrichment program was even worse. He became frightened on the bus ride over and again refused to get off the bus, crying and protesting all the way. To add to Jamie's stresses, the family had recently moved, necessitating a longer commute for his parents and taking more time away from him.

As we worked together on the adoption related aspects of his behavior, it became clear he was terrified of being left, of being abandoned, of being lost in a way where he would not be found. Fortunately though, Jamie was in a school environment that was also very concerned and open to understanding separation issues. They were willing to do whatever was necessary and feasible to help him master this stage of development.

His mother began to work with him very specifically on the nature of his fears and as he began to tell her what he imagined might happen, he began to find the school adjustment a bit easier. Since he was a bright and articulate child he was able to communicate that he needed more time alone with her, and she was able to find a way to provide it which increased his ability to cope. If school personnel and parent input had been less than optimal, Jamie might have needed to wait another year before starting kindergarten. He might have needed to do this under any circumstances and delay this step into the more demanding world of formal schooling. Even so, a careful eye to separation issues will be important in Jamie's world for many years. At each stage of development, it will again become a critical issue.

Though Bethany appeared to be ready for school at the appropriate time, she still expressed her reluctance to be separated from her mother. Part of the answer to her stealing and lying may have come from the need to have more private time with Sara and a chance to work on developing a bond with her mother that was so affected by the critical timing of the separation from her foster mother at the age of seven months. Perhaps Sara's feeling that Bethany was trying to fill a void in herself was a reflection of serious attachment issues as well as the possibility of some additional unknown genetic components created by prenatal factors which exist for some children. According to Janelle Peterson (see Chapter 2) behaviors linked almost exclusively to Reactive Attachment Disorder (RAD) children are stealing or hoarding of food and chronic or nonsensical lying, even when these children are faced with the truth or caught in the act.

If the child has learned how to master impulses and substitute thought for action, she will be able to fulfill requirements made of her during school hours when she is away from home. This ability will probably be determined by her organic endowment as the push towards need oriented behavior becomes less urgent and the ability to think and wait becomes more possible. It should be kept in mind that regression occurs legitimately from time to time in normal development.

Controls will sometimes be temporarily lost after they have been achieved, and it is best if these regressions are not met by disapproval if they are to give way to forward movement. The child's personality is expected to be unpredictable due to the uneven movement along development lines. Knowing this, it is easier to understand the natural disequilibrium of the young child and the infinite variations of normality. Clearly, the intricacy of this process makes an assessment for kindergarten of critical importance and should be left in the hands of a skilled evaluator.

Another of the important aspects of assessing a child's readiness for kindergarten and elementary school is understanding the level of development of her thinking processes. Jean Piaget devoted his life's work to understanding how a child's mind develops, what she can learn at what stage and how best to teach under these circumstances. In *Piaget in the Classroom* (1973), we are told that the thought processes of young children are completely different from those of adults. At some time, between ages four and eight, there is a drastic change in their thinking as they acquire the ability for reversibility, which means being able to shift from one particular point of view to another. Now they have the capacity to see that an object can be seen several different ways and still maintain its reliability as a permanent object.

In order for this maturation in thinking to progress, the child must have what psychologists term "object permanency." Object permanence is the internalized picture of the mother or primary attachment figure and the belief that this figure is trustworthy and permanent. It is at this stage, as the child interacts with people and things, that she discovers links between events. She can now see that she can cancel out one action and perform another. In order to do this, it becomes clear to the researcher that time and the experiences of daily living are the essentials that help a child transition from early to mid-childhood thinking. If something has happened in the child's early life to stop that trust from developing, then object permanency will be threatened and normal development may not proceed. If we think back to Bethany's early life, we can see that the bond between mother and child had been broken twice, and she and her family were now living with its consequences.

As Piaget tells us, a child at around six or seven, begins to realize she can mentally stop actions and shift from one idea to another. She now gradually becomes capable of taking a point of view other than her own and understanding someone else's feelings and thoughts, furthering the bond between parent and child. If the child's sense of survival is impaired, this shift in thinking ability will be very hard to achieve.

We do not yet completely understand how language is acquired and how representation and symbolization develop. We do know that at this age children learn by looking and listening and when they combine this new information with what they already have, there is a strong possibility for the child to misunderstand. According to Piaget, information coming from outside is taken in and interfaced with knowledge the child already possesses. Out of this interactive process, the mistakes and misinterpretations the child makes can be understood. Due to this discovery, many professionals believe that every effort should be made to help each child develop his unique and fundamental abilities for thinking.

For adopted children there are two or three very important truths to be gleaned from Piaget's works. Before learning can proceed, object permanence must be achieved. When the child has had to change parents, her ability to attach and to move towards object permanence has been interrupted and she either cannot reattach or will be slowed in this process, creating a gap between her chronological age and the age at which she is operating developmentally. This may result in her not being ready for early schooling, nursery or kindergarten, as other children her age would be. Because her parents often do not have the benefit of genetic background information it is very difficult to anticipate if there are learning disabilities, or if the child has ADD, or other conditions passed on by birth parents that compound her inability to form object permanence. Whatever disabilities or conditions she has will affect the learning process.

This child would probably benefit from more time at home with the consistent presence of her parent thereby avoiding another separation. She may, however, be in a family in which there is no possibility that one parent can stay home even as long as Sara was able to with Bethany, necessitating the presence of more than one caregiver or an early day care or school experience. With these conditions in mind, it will be important for the adoptive parents to spend as much time as possible with their children, and provide as many experiences of doing and seeing and interacting as possible in order to facilitate the development of the thinking process and build object constancy. Looking for early signs of developmental delay and being emotionally prepared that their child may not be ready for school experiences at the expected age can lead parents toward constructive measures.

The elementary school years for adopted children are of great importance. Adopted children may not be able to think in a way that helps them explore some of the very deep and puzzling feelings they have about themselves and their lives. Lois Melina (see Chapter 4) helps us understand the adoption thoughts and feelings of the child at this age. The child may begin to wonder why her birth parents placed her for adoption and what they were like. Perhaps she will feel sad or angry, and begin to grieve for the lost possibilities for understanding her origins and the people who brought her into the world.

Adoption issues are complicated and can be overwhelming for the child in these years as she tries to sort through her feelings about them. She needs help from her adoptive parents and perhaps from mental health professionals. One of the most prevalent and hurtful beliefs on the part of the child is her idea that her birthmother abandoned her because she was undesirable in some way. It is hard to understand, but important to hear that the birthmother was not able to parent any child at that time in her life when she gave up her child for adoption. Bethany was not in touch with any of these feelings at this age. In fact, Bethany had stated the opposite—that she was very happy to be adopted and very lucky. Most likely, she had pushed all such feelings aside and perhaps did not even realize that they were there.

Children between the ages of seven and eleven mature a great deal. Their reasoning becomes more complex and advanced. They can now think in more complicated ways about their beginnings and their birth parents. It is a time for sharing letters and belongings from birth parents and expanding on the simple story they were told as young children. The fantasies about birth parents will become more complex and usually characterize the birth parents as larger than life—famous or rich or certainly more desirable than the adoptive parents, or conversely, evil and frightening, too horrible to even imagine. This is not unlike the fantasies that are common among most children, but, in this case, they are more fully developed and grounded in some reality. For adopted children, there actually is a second set of parents while, for most children, there is only the fantasy.

Grieving plays a significant role for the adopted child in the early school years. Her feelings are often intense, as she becomes aware that she has lost her birth family—people extremely significant in her life. She mourns for that loss and moves through the stages of grieving in a rather predictable pattern. She may not want her adoptive parents to know she is sad for fear of hurting them. She may wish she could be born to the parents she lives with and avoid the burden and the complexity of having to deal with adoption.

The cost of repressing this grief can be high, creating emotional and behavioral problems. What is important during this stage is to look for signs of grieving or sadness, to acknowledge these feelings and to help the child try to make sense of it all and move past this stage for now, until it comes again in the next cycle of working it through. Grieving over a lost life is unavoidable and to deny it, cover it up, or judge it will not help the child to learn to factor this set of circumstances into her understanding of her life story.

Adoptive parents should be aware that their children may have some troublesome notions to deal with. Among them is the one that tells them that they are not as good as other people because they are adopted, or that they must achieve in order to keep their parents' love and not be rejected, or that they will surely be separated from their adoptive parents, repeating a pattern experienced earlier in life. Certainly, the self-esteem issues Bethany struggled with highlight an additional developmental line for her and for all adopted children complicating their lives and making the road to maturity and independence more difficult than the one traveled by children in traditional families.

Melina strongly suggests making a life book with an adopted child at this age, chronicling all the important activities and events and memories that have occurred. This is the story of her life and should be a shared activity between parent and child, as a way of giving proper respect to her birth, her growth and development, her ideas, her activities, and her hopes for the future. To some degree, Bethany was asking for help when she went to John and Sara about her concerns around the time of Lisa Steinberg's tragic death and when she asked Sara if Sara could stay home instead of work. Although they responded in an appropriate and sensitive way, it might have been even more helpful if they had extended their response by engaging Bethany in making a life book, allowing her to verbalize and clarify some of the complicated thoughts and feelings she must have been having about adoption at that time in her life. This activity might have encouraged her to tell them about some of the long held ideas she had about adoption that she had kept to herself or hadn't even thought to share since they were so familiar to her.

The early school years are an intense and potentially fruitful time for parenting an adopted child. Growth is accelerated and a great deal is happening in the development of the thinking process. Feelings become more complex, and the child is rapidly becoming an integrated, recognizably unique individual. It is a time for capitalizing on every possible avenue for helping the child solidify attachment and become centered in the world.

6

ON THE EDGE: THE MIDDLE SCHOOL YEARS

Though our intuition told us that something wasn't right, it was hard to argue with,
"I am doing my work. If I wasn't, don't you think you would hear from the teacher?"

Much is made of the adolescent in middle school. "The kids are really acting crazy then," I was told repeatedly. But as a middle school teacher, I saw it differently. My experience was that most young people entering their new school were at a delightful stage of development. This was a wondrous time for them, right before they developed into teenage cynics, and they were still excited by new ideas and the wonder of learning. For most, it was exhilarating to receive praise from their teachers, and they were energized as they competed with their friends in showing how clever they were. It made for a stimulating classroom and assured that most of the students were attentive and engaged in learning.

I had always assumed that my children would fit this profile as we had spent their early years preparing them for a lifetime of ideas and thought. We were a family of readers; we loved to discuss ideas; we traveled, went to the theater and concerts. Large family gatherings were spent discussing literature and reviewing the world situation. We were sure that we were helping them to develop a love of knowledge and intellectual pursuits. How could we miss?

But teaching introduced me to a small group of students in middle school who were slowly giving up on their intellectual development. They took no pleasure in school work, either refusing to do it or doing it in such a slap-hazard fashion that they might as well not have done it at all. I viewed this as sad and unfortunate and, obviously, the result of inadequate parental motivation. These were the children, I smugly assumed, whose parents never read or discussed ideas with them nor helped them to set standards for their adult lives. How easy it is to be so smart!

I remember one meeting with the parents of a very bright, but unmotivated young man. He was frequently absent or late for school. Most of his assignments were handed in way past their due date if they were done at all. In the mornings, he would linger in bed not wanting to get up and come to school. His mother's approach alternated between screaming at him to get up or giving up and just letting him sleep through the morning.

"What do you mean you can't get him to do his homework and get up for school? You're the parent," I reminded them. How I would eat my words just a short time later! Here was one of many widely accepted myths that I would have to give up: children flourish when their parents are involved in their lives.

When Bethany began middle school, we were gratified that she appeared to be doing well, both academically and socially. In sixth grade, she had perfect school attendance, a perfect homework record, and her report cards reflected mostly excellent performances. Test scores when carefully scrutinized however, showed another point of view. They ranged from the 99th percentile in Number Concepts to the 30th percentile in Language Expression. The interpreters of the test considered the Language result average; we did not. The 30th percentile meant that she was expressing herself better than 30 percent of youngsters her age, but conversely, it meant that she was performing the same skill at a level below 70 percent of the same population. That is not average. We were surprised. Her lowest scores were in Listening, Language Mechanics and Language Expression. Unaware that this could be pointing to a significant deficit, we focused on what our experience had shown us, and there had never been indications of learning problems. In fact, Bethany had learned to speak early and well. As a very young child, she showed an unusual ability to think abstractly and to figure things out.

Since her performance in school was so good and her teachers were pleased with her work, we decided not to focus on the gap in the scores. Instead, we would weigh the classroom achievement more heavily than the results of one test, since these tests are often taken under stress and indicative of circumstances peculiar to one particular day. So here it was that we were given our first tangible sign that Bethany may have had a subtle reading and/or language problem. That we chose to ignore it, I can now see, turned out to have important implications in a short time to come. In our defense, this is seen only in hindsight and without the benefit of any teacher or evaluator helping us to understand it. In regard to the school, Bethany was performing optimally, both socially and academically.

Middle school age is the time that young adolescents test their developing independence. Choosing their own friends, scheduling their free time, selecting their own clothes, however it is framed, independence is the driving force. For our daughter, we thought we had been preparing the way for her to develop that independence. Having an allowance and providing her with opportunities to earn additional money gave her many occasions to thoughtfully form choices. We saw this as training her to make mature decisions throughout her life. At dinnertime, many discussions centered on decision-making and how to formulate reasoned choices using our own lives and the lives of acquaintances as starting points. Even sitcom and movie and book characters provided opportunities for examination, but I do recall Bethany's lack of attentiveness to many of these talks. She'd try to distract us from the discussion by changing the subject, cracking jokes, or responding to a question with a bewildered "huh?" as if she didn't understand. We puzzled over these responses, but could not understand what was happening or why. So we explained it away as a phase Bethany was going through, instead of looking further at the hints that appeared in her school test results.

For most youngsters at this stage, especially girls, their search for autonomy is intimately involved with their social group. As they assert their independence from their parents, they become more dependent upon their peers. Growing up means fitting in and adapting themselves to their friends' values and lifestyles. Wearing the right clothes, using the right jargon, behaving in the accepted way often takes precedence over their school life as they rush towards adulthood.

Bethany was no different in this respect. Her social life became more and more dominant, and her educational time retreated into the background. Entering puberty early had not provided her with any advantages either. Often she was the recipient of suggestive stares from older boys and even men. Though appearing older, she was still clearly emotionally immature and easily distracted from her schoolwork. The phone rang incessantly. She spent hours talking with friends. Several times a day she would change her clothes, and she refused to wear any that did not have the currently prized designer label. But despite what we saw as indifference to her schoolwork, she continued to bring home adequate report cards and positive comments from her teachers.

In seventh grade, Bethany began to play soccer and she loved it. She had a good relationship with the coach and enjoyed the aggressiveness of the sport. She was a good player helping to lead her team in an undefeated season. Academically, her marks ranged from good to excellent, but at home we had a hard time tracking her work. When we asked to see her homework, she would tell us that she had done it at school and left her books in her locker. When questioned about her reading, she assured us she was doing her required work. Discussions about the books, however, were vague, no specific references to actual content. We waited for contact from teachers about her participation, but no calls or letters came. When I called to find out if she was meeting her obligations, I got no negative reports, only comments that perhaps I was being too overbearing, so we backed off and assumed that she was telling us the truth.

Socially, she seemed well liked by everyone. It was only at the end of the year with the final report card that we now saw from the teachers' comments that her effort and performance in several classes had been inconsistent. Why had we not been told about this before, especially in light of our phone calls to the teachers? Her marks had fallen from the previous year by at least a letter grade in each course. Where there had been Es there were now Gs; where there were pluses there were now minuses. And her test scores in many areas had declined from 5 to 20 percentile points in almost every area. Throughout the year, she had managed to squeak by. Not being grossly inattentive, appearing to be polite and respectful had been a shield for her lack of motivation and enthusiasm for her studies. Concerned but not anxious, we decided to be more attentive the following year and monitor her homework and progress more closely. What we could do about the apathy surrounding her schoolwork was a puzzle.

In eighth grade, we continued to see credible marks, but we still saw no evidence that she was doing any work. I could tell from my discussions with her that she wasn't reading the books that were assigned, and I suspected that she was probably relying on her friends to help her complete her assignments. I tried to set aside time to read together but she was so slippery, and there were still no danger signals coming from school. Her marks were good and the response was always the same. Condescendingly, I was told to back off and not put so much pressure on her. "Other parents would be thrilled to have a child who was doing so well." Perhaps they knew something. Perhaps she was a star in school and just playing a game at home. I wanted so much to believe them and her that I tried to ignore my doubts.

But the doubts didn't go away. Every time I had a conversation with a friend about their children's participation in school it brought them right back. I would hear about book reports, research projects, portfolios, debates, and forums, all the things that I was involved in at my work. Bethany never mentioned any of these. And I knew her schoolwork should be getting more lengthy and complex as she headed toward high school, but the opposite seemed to be happening. She was doing less and less.

Our common sense told us that something wasn't right, but it was hard to argue with. "I am doing my work. If I wasn't, don't you think you would hear from my teachers?" Bethany would reply. We awaited a phone call or a letter from school, but with no such feedback and with decent report cards, we had nowhere to go with our concerns. I felt like I was losing control. Who could we turn to? It's hard to say to a teacher, "Why is she getting a 90 in your class? She's not doing the work or reading any books or writing any papers."

Because of her high math scores, Bethany had been placed in an advanced math course. Just two years before, Johns Hopkins had highlighted her as "gifted in math." But soon after the first semester when she earned a 79, she complained that the work was too difficult. In actuality, she wasn't doing any work. She wanted it to come to her immediately and effortlessly without the drill or practice that homework provides. Homework, as she saw it, should be done in class while the teacher was talking. Until then this approach had worked, and she had been able to get good marks. Against our wishes, she dropped the advanced class and with a minimal amount of work, she received a 96 in regular math. The lesson she came away with was the opposite of what we wanted: taking the easy way out was reinforced for her. "See, I am in the right class!" she boasted. Whereas, we had been trying to instill a commitment to hard work and pride in the struggle, her reality was teaching her just the opposite—all you need to do is get by.

Unfortunately, Bethany now began to develop a secret life, one that took place away from us in the company of new friends. Though we tried to maintain control of her after school time, scheduling art lessons and sports activities, she would often skip these to hang out with people we did not know. She and her art teacher began to clash because of her erratic attendance, and Bethany ultimately dropped her class. She had given up music lessons the year before. All that was left was soccer which, fortunately, she still enjoyed and excelled in.

It was also in eighth grade that we believe she started drinking alcohol and smoking pot, not uncommon among many teenagers today. The guidance counselor called to tell us that Bethany and a few of her friends had been caught drinking during lunchtime. The friends confessed, but Bethany insisted that she had only been an observer. Perhaps, perhaps not, but the school, represented by the counselor, considered the incident serious enough to call us in for a meeting and to recommend that we take her to a therapist. Confused as to why they would make such a recommendation if they did not believe she was guilty, we tried to pin them down. Were there other incidents? Had she been having trouble in any classes, with any teachers, with other students? The answer was an emphatic "no," but nevertheless, the recommendation was loud and clear. "We think Bethany should get some counseling."

It was our impression that of the five students involved, the recommendation for counseling was made only for her, but there were no specific details forthcoming from anyone as to why she was being singled out. These were mixed signals we were getting. On the one hand we were hearing, "She's doing fine," and on the other hand, "We think she needs counseling." The possibility of learning disabilities did not come up in any discussion with the school. There were many references made to Bethany's superior intelligence and disappointing choices. We tried to fill in the missing pieces but left the office even more bewildered. What weren't we being told? Was this a justification of all of our old fears: her lack of effort, her inability to make moral choices, her attempts to get attention through negative behavior? We did not minimize the school's concerns. They were our concerns too.

The outcome of that meeting was to send Bethany to her second therapist. The school had given us a list of counselors who worked with adolescents. This time we chose a therapist who had trained at a facility that focused on teenagers with substance abuse problems. John and I agreed that we needed guidance in bringing her through this difficult stage. Maybe someone else could help us to reinforce stable and mature decision-making processes and help Bethany redirect herself and develop healthy goals. The subject of adoption was skimmed over by everyone as we all assumed that we were dealing with exaggerated adolescent turmoil.

In counseling, our daughter spent her hours being charming and chatty, giving little truth of herself and her life and providing little insight. The therapist was clearly confused by the differing stories he heard, one from Bethany who said how great her life was and one from us in which we spoke of our fears for her. In addition to telling him about the stealing and lying, we presented a child who refused to try for the excellence that she was so capable of achieving. Our experiences had taught us that the best rewards we get in life were the ones we gave ourselves for a job well done. Bethany was denying herself these dividends.

At this time, she was beginning to have problems socially. She reported to us that former friends were snubbing her or saying hurtful things, and she became the frequent victim of threatening and prank phone calls. I knew that something she was doing was engendering this behavior from older girls in the community, and when I tried to discuss it with her I was told, "They think I'm trying to steal their boyfriends just because they like to talk to me."

As onlookers we thought she might be misreading social signals and in her craving to be "popular" was setting herself up for victimization. Our discussions with her went nowhere. So, we crossed our fingers hoping that there were productive discussions between her and the therapist.

The phone calls continued and sometimes they contained threats of physical violence. Bethany responded with macho bravado, "Just let 'em try. I'll get my friends to beat their asses!" What friends? The old friends I knew were all in the library doing their homework or playing soccer on the ball field. I didn't know the new ones. She was becoming a magnet for conflict, and her secret life was expanding. I could feel her pulling away from us and the security of her family toward an unhealthy place filled with conflict and disharmony.

As all this was happening, we also observed Bethany's behavior becoming more frenzied. The little girl who didn't like to be held or pursue quiet activities was approaching her teenage years constantly in motion. She raced from one activity to another with little time to enjoy one before she moved on to the next. She had two long-standing friends who shared this frantic behavior with her. Both from privileged families, attractive and bright, the girls seemed to feed on each other's negative behavior. Often Bethany would arrive home at the end of a day with them, cigarette burns on her arms. "Someone threw a cigarette out of the car window, and it flew in the back and burned me," was the first response to our query. Then, "Jamie burned me by accident." Finally her explanation was, "Alexis wanted to see who would scream first." We were horrified. This was our daughter. How could this be happening? This kind of behavior was so alien to us, contrary to anything we had ever seen or participated in. We could not help but project into the future where we envisioned a lifetime of abuse for our baby girl. What did this say about her and the choices she was making? What did it say about our ability to parent her and to help her develop into a confident person? Rational discussions were met with disdain and stony silences. We reported the behavior to the therapist who questioned her. "Oh my parents. They worry about everything. We were just fooling around."

The proverbial image of a roller coaster comes to mind. Slowly it moves to the peak of its climb. When it reaches the top its descent is fast and furious and there is no way to stop it. I was terrified that Bethany was on the back of that roller coaster ride as it was making its way up the slope before it began that frenzied ride down.

The school year ended and her report card indicated none of this. All of her marks, except one, were in the 90s, so we again scratched our heads wondering if we were crazy and looked toward the following year when she would begin high school and hopefully would have matured over the summer.

Bethany had one onerous challenge to accomplish before she would begin high school. At the end of the summer, she was scheduled to have surgery for a congenital bone malformation in her jaw. It was an extensive procedure and involved a lengthy recuperation which would delay her entrance into the new school for several weeks.

As the surgeon described the operation in detail she asked few questions while my head felt like a leaded weight was attached to it. When asked if she understood, her easy "sure" belied the feelings that I knew must be stuffed somewhere in the back of her mind. So surmising that she might be trying to protect me from her fears, I asked the doctor to explain it to her in private, hoping that she would ask him for information. Instead she gave me a, "Mom, don't you think I would ask if I had any questions? If it has to be done it has to be done. What's the use of talking about it?" So there!

Should I applaud her bravery or worry about the unspoken feelings. I did both at alternate times, in silence and in discussion with John and friends. It certainly wasn't the way I would react if I was in her place, but I had never felt the need to play the tough young woman.

In preparation for her surgery, Bethany had four wisdom teeth removed during the spring. It was like a dress rehearsal, for here too, she never complained or expressed any fear. In contrast, I had been a nervous wreck preparing myself for the worst. Now she was heading for the operating room, and I could barely contain my apprehension. The surgeon was going to break her jaw, push it forward and wire her mouth shut for four to six weeks. She would wake up in the ICU swollen and drugged and in the days that followed would have to take nourishment through a straw, and she would be unable to talk. This would terrify most people, but stalwart Bethany was mute about the upcoming ordeal.

The rest of the summer that she planned was a varied one. Two weeks on a bike trip on Cape Cod with old friends from camp and then two weeks at soccer camp. We were pleased with her choices; they involved strenuous exercise and hard work with, we were sure, emotional dividends for the effort. But Bethany was who she was. Although told to prepare for the physical rigors of the biking trip, she chose to hang out with friends instead and so was unprepared for the strenuous daily trek. Though she managed to stick it out, it was difficult. In our phone calls, she expressed little enthusiasm for the adventure.

The two-week soccer camp did not go so well either. At the end of the fourth day, she called to ask us to pick her up early and, clever that she was, told us it was because she couldn't deal with all of the religious "stuff" associated with the camp. We were a family with mixed religious backgrounds and had introduced the kids to several religions, but had intentionally stayed away from what we perceived as the dogma and ceremony implied by affiliation with one religion. We raised Matt and Bethany with what we believed were high moral standards and respect for all traditions. In retrospect, I now believe that the discipline of religious training, the clarity of moral issues might have shielded her from the enormity of the choices which she confronted each day. But at that time, Bethany pushed the right button. We hadn't signed her on for religious education. It was soccer she had wanted and we had agreed to, so we consented to let her come home early. Later I wondered if she had even been telling us the truth and why I hadn't called the camp for an explanation. I think I subconsciously wanted to spend more time with her before she went into the hospital, so I accepted her story without question.

Unbeknownst to us, Bethany had been making new friends that last year, and they had played a role in diverting her attention from her after school activities. By coming home early from soccer camp, she was able to have additional time to spend with these new friends, and we were now getting little inklings that these were not good relationships. We soon became aware of names and faces that we could associate with a group of young people hanging around town as they killed time waiting.

"What for?" I wondered. For the summer to pass? For life to begin? For something of interest to pass by?

We were not inspired. But Bethany was attracted to what she perceived as their independence with a touch of wildness and daring. I tried to distract her with a variety of activities, but she clamored to go into town to be with these friends. So we worked out some compromises and divided the time between my planned activities and her hanging out time with her new group. It was right before the surgery! How could I say, "No?" She needed friends, I believed, to help her through her imminent ordeal.

And where was Matt when this was all happening? He too had been away for most of the summer, doing volunteer work out west. "Silent Matt," we called him. Like the proverbial monkeys, he would see no evil, hear no evil and speak no evil. He stayed out of his sister's personal life, rarely commenting on what he saw or informing us about the goings on, so we had no hints at home about Bethany's secret life. To us, the kids still appeared to be very close, but later we learned that there was a separation developing between them. Whereas before they had been best friends and spent a lot of time at home together, Bethany was now transferring her attention to this new group while Matt found them crude and unpleasant.

Matt's development was very different from his sister's. Unlike Bethany, he was reserved. He had a hard time talking to people he didn't know well, teachers, his peers, and even relatives. Despite this, he was well liked by everyone: the nerds, the bullies, and the jocks. He had a great sense of humor and was very calm and even-tempered, but he was so shy that he didn't have really close friends, except for some he had made at camp who lived a few hours away from us. His shyness prevented him from being included in many social events, and he was unhappy about this. He spent a lot of time alone with his thoughts and his projects. He drew, made constructions, read, mostly comics, took walks in the woods and was interested in many subjects. He had been first place winner in a school wide Geography Bee and though his marks were indifferent because he was unmotivated, he absorbed almost all of what he heard. He presented himself as thoughtful, balanced and non-judgmental with a winning sense of humor.

Three weeks passed quickly. As they wheeled her on the gurney to her surgery it was she who comforted me. "Don't worry Mom. They do this operation all the time," she said. "I'm going to be all right. Tell Matt and Dad I said 'hey!'"

"Oh my God," I thought. "I should be comforting her, and she is consoling me." I silently made all kinds of bargains to affirm the truth in her words. I wept that my child was making such a valiant effort to calm me and presenting this strong facade in the face of her fear. It was ironic that just a few hours ago she had been pushing me away. Now there was this sudden shift! Later I could see this for what it really was—another way for her to build a barrier between her and her feelings.

I remember the family waiting room outside of the ICU unit. We waited along with the family and friends of a young man dying of AIDS. The tragedy of his death made my vigil seem trivial, and yet I was terrified. What if something went wrong? I'm sure I needn't go into detail over the agonizing I did as I sat there alone in my thoughts. Among my fantasies was the fear that if something went wrong I would have to explain it to Bethany's birthmother. So many times over the years, I had thought about this unknown woman. This surgery, though undertaken to make our daughter's life better, was still elective. What if we had made the wrong choice?

But fortunately, she was okay. My first visit to the ICU unit showed her with cheeks swollen to the size of small melons. She could barely move; neither one of us could talk. A nurse gave her a pad and pencil and in her limited scrawl she wrote: "I ♥ U." The tears crawled down my face as I silently celebrated her survival.

In the family waiting room, the surgeon was elated. Never had such a procedure gone so smoothly. Everything went better than expected; in fact, it went so well that, "We didn't even have to wire her mouth shut. She'll be just fine as soon as the swelling goes down."

John and I were jubilant. We had prepared ourselves for every possibility except this one. "It went better than expected." An overnight in the hospital for both of us; a weekend in bed and a few days out of school and she would be better than new. "Take her to the orthodontist in two weeks for a checkup." Well, that was the schedule we followed, and Bethany returned to school in about a week, and one week later, she went to her orthodontist for the mandatory exam.

"Oops!"

"Oops?"

To my mind that sound, it's not even a word, has only one meaning. Some horrible mistake has happened, and that's exactly what this was. Her jaw had slid right back into its old position and it was already setting. In not wiring the mouth shut, the doctor had allowed it to return to its former condition, something that probably could have been predicted. Bethany would have to endure almost the entire procedure again.

Did she scream? Did she curse? Cry? Blame? No, not even at this point. I could barely look at her. I felt so awful. I had chosen the doctor. I had encouraged her to have the surgery. But it was she who would have to bear the burden of the doctor's mistake. Her only concession to her anger was her desire to sue him, a plan of action suggested to her by her friends, I am sure. But she controlled her anger denying herself an outlet for her feelings and us the chance to nurture and comfort her.

Bethany was in the nurse's office at school. This was a place she knew well and often went with vague physical complaints. The nurse called home to say that Bethany wasn't feeling well and perhaps John, who frequently worked from the house, could pick her up and take her home. He spoke to her, and they decided that she would rest for a half-hour and then see if she felt any better. Immediately after hanging up, the surgeon's office called to tell us to bring her to the hospital right away; they would do the surgery the next day. When John showed up she was surprised that he had changed his mind, but even more surprised to find out she was going to the hospital. None of us had thought the surgery would be scheduled so quickly. Some might think this was good, less time to worry, but I believe, in this case, she was thrown off balance and left with another reason not to trust. The adults had not prepared her for such swift action, and I am sure she felt betrayed. This time the recovery was longer, and she was home for several weeks. None of the new friends visited or called. We hoped they were gone for good, temporary buddies who had helped her through a difficult time. In all, we were at the end of October when she finally returned to school.

We were worried about Bethany, but hoped that the anticipation of her surgery and her inability to express her feelings was what had been holding her back. We hoped that now she could make a fresh start and that her life would flourish.

Why weren't we worried about Matt? Shy—having few friends—not thriving in school? What was the difference? The difference was that he had interests; he told us what was on his mind, what was bothering him. He didn't leave the room when one of us came in. He didn't distance himself, but participated in the family life, cooking meals, hanging out, watching films, talking to us. Like Bethany he was not thrilled with his life, but he had interests that engaged him and didn't appear to be conflicted about who he was.

◆   ◆   ◆

A period of relative calm and integration commonly called preadolescence occurs directly prior to puberty and the beginning of adolescence proper. Erik H. Erikson (1968), an eminent psychoanalyst, scholar, and author has offered extensive knowledge that helps us understand the developmental tasks to be mastered during this important phase. Mastering these tasks is essential in providing a solid footing for entering puberty and the middle school years.

Erikson describes school as being a world unto itself with its own goals, achievements, disappointments and limitations. During the preadolescent years, there is a need to develop a sense of industry, to learn to make things and make them well. What is at stake is the development and maintenance in children of a positive identification with those who know things and know how to do things. What is at risk during the preadolescent years is the danger that a child will not achieve enjoyment from work or pride in doing something really well.

The structure of a culture must reach into school life and support in every child a feeling of competence. This achievement is critical for developing a lasting and gratifying basis for cooperative participation in adult life. It is possible at this stage to learn to be overly rigid in responsibility and have a sense of duty without enough joy, or on the other hand, to learn to focus only on doing what one wants to do. Indeed, there is a third possibility which is to feel overwhelmed and not up to mastering the tasks of this stage of development which often leads to avoidance and depression.

Just as we are hoping that a feeling of competence has developed for the child in regard to work, puberty arrives, childhood comes to an end, and the challenge of the middle school years begins. The age at which puberty is recognized depends on the culture in which it is taking place, but the universal criterion is physical development.

For most youngsters, a rapid growth spurt, such as usually occurs at puberty, can bring with it a troublesome psychological state, since it is quite difficult to cope with so much change in a short period of time. Equilibrium is lost at puberty leading to the well-known 7th or 8th grade slump. That Bethany was not striving for excellence in school was indicative of this stage and could have been initially understood as her response to early puberty.

In our culture, puberty itself is a crisis and often a crisis of considerable proportion. Most adolescents experience episodes of disturbed behavior intermingled with periods of relative stability. There are identity issues involving identity loss, identity confusion, and sometimes an identity crisis.

Another adolescent pattern involves prolonged disruptive experiences with persistent conflicts that may become a way of life. These youngsters will have difficulty developing a strong conscience and conforming to the rules of society. Other individuals remain, however, in a fixed, emotionally immature state. These are the ones who do not go through real, constructive developmental changes such as normally occur in adolescence. This state of affairs usually does eventually terminate; however, long-term problems will remain and become evident if development remains static at this stage. These individuals will present as weak and indecisive personalities.

There is at puberty a preoccupation with the body due to radically changing body proportions and a surge of sexual and aggressive energies. As this is happening, the young adolescent may also be withdrawing from her parents and their influences toward other interests and a stronger connection with the peer group. While this serves positive purposes for the maturation process, allowing for the loosening of old patterns in order for better, more adult ones to emerge, it also causes a withdrawal reaction. It is not unusual for a teenager to feel threatened and confused. Just when she needs help, she loses the internal perception of having parental support which is so important to her stability. Often a young person at this time will experience a mourning stage accompanied by moodiness and a heightened sense of emptiness, loneliness, and isolation.

While all adolescents experience ongoing tension from the inner struggle between the need to remain a child and the need to grow up, for some this struggle can take a more disconcerting form than for others. Some may withdraw into adolescent rebellion, rejecting parental values and trying to fill the void with drugs, alcohol or food as well as intimate physical relationships with peers. For others, the unwillingness to assume independence and growing responsibilities is expressed by holding onto immature behaviors such as baby talk, playing with age inappropriate toys and over dependence on parental direction. Either choice can create considerable conflict at home.

At this time, it is typical that nothing the parents do or say is acceptable, and the child is questioning the reliability of her parent's beliefs and values. This questioning is often accompanied by crushes on various other adults, probably as a way of reducing interest in the parents.

In puberty, the highest level of abstract thinking surfaces preparing the way for adult decision-making. There is also a consuming interest in everything sexual and a wide range of behaviors towards sex, most usually followed by a move towards dating that is typically established by mid-adolescence. Behavior and attitudes are unpredictable and experimental, and there is often rebellion and an intense self-centeredness.

In adolescence, action can be a means of avoiding these inner conflicts and can thus delay maturation by interfering with intellectual development and learning. Action, for its own sake, may become predominant, marked by over impulsivity and a failure of inner controls. At this point, action can become a substitute for thought, and there is the danger of the development of psychopathology or delinquency.

At this age, youngsters form cliques of all types to test the capacity for maintaining loyalties to friends, as well as to find security in group support and affirmation. For some adolescents, impaired in their ability to "make it" in the peer group due to poor adaptive skills, there is a tendency to band together as outsiders.

Early adolescence is a particularly vulnerable time for developing at risk behavior. It is now taken for granted that most young teens will be smoking and perhaps drinking in their free time. It is common knowledge that there is widespread use of substance in middle school. The selling of drugs in and around school buildings even during class has been documented. It is just at this moment that intervention by a therapist, sports coach or activity leader is critical to guide these young people in positive directions where they can find ways to achieve, believe in themselves, and combat the forces of a negative group process. Adolescents are looking for ideas and people to trust who can provide them with models outside the family.

The beginnings of rituals, signaling the move towards adulthood, now appear. Youngsters view age thirteen as the magic number that marks the beginning of their teens. At thirteen, young adolescents from a variety of religious backgrounds are participating in ceremonies that recognize the beginning of adult status.

Cultures vary widely in their definition of adulthood. In primitive cultures, the end of adolescence is recognized by a ritual event, marking the start of adulthood with all of its responsibilities and privileges. In this country, we have two major criteria for defining adulthood: the ability to earn one's living and the other which involves a contemporary rite of passage such as voting, driving, and legal drinking. However, at this particular time in our culture a young person may not be an economically self-sufficient adult until she reaches her thirties.

Adolescents in our culture find it very difficult to live by the culturally expected sexual morality and often pay a high price for attempting to do so. Often at puberty and throughout adolescence, sexual urges are intense and at times appear to be almost obsessive. This biological circumstance is coupled with the delayed ability to pair off, establish family life, and assume the role of adults, due to an increased need to get advanced education. Since there are fewer and fewer jobs for unskilled and semi-skilled labor, especially at incomes that adequately cover the costs of family life, young people are placed in the position of needing to acquire a substantial education or else manage on a substandard annual wage. This forces most of them to postpone becoming wage earners, requiring them to remain dependent on others financially and often delaying maturity. There is indeed a wide gap between the biological coming of age and the socioeconomic ability to assume the adult role in our culture, creating important identity incongruities.

In today's culture, families often have two working parents. This creates another social pressure that starts to show its effects by the middle school years. Confusion can develop about specifically defined gender roles such as childcare and household and income issues. The development of a stable sexual identity becomes a more difficult process for the child. If the adults are clear about their roles, there is little reason for this confusion to develop, but if the adults feel conflicted, or if there is tension around these issues, adolescents will be more likely to reject their parents' lifestyle choices, since accepting them does not feel safe. In truth, children may want their mothers to be home for them, as Bethany described in her dream, but the financial pressures of modern life often make this choice unavailable.

Today, adolescent and mainstream culture in our society is changing so rapidly that those now providing the role models for young teens are often older siblings, pop stars and sports figures, as well as parents. The fashion and entertainment industries have gained wide acceptance as trendsetters, exerting undo influence over young people's thinking, behavior, and taste in clothing and music. Moreover, adolescents today define themselves by their dress and taste in music, which represent for them, a particular posture and ideology.

Adolescents may experience intense anxiety and express it in profound ways. Reckless and impulsive behavior of all kinds, including substance abuse, sexual confusion, experimentation and delinquency are common at this age. Such behavior understandably stirs up anxiety and alarm in parents and adults in general, in ways that make this an unusually challenging stage of life for all concerned.

The first phase of adolescence ends in the middle teens. The physiological changes which signal the beginning of adolescence stabilize somewhere around this time, while the psychological responses will not fully stabilize until later. Among those teens who struggle the most are those who have likely had developmental problems occurring during the time of the bonding cycle or during prenatal development. As previously described, this situation could have developed as a result of such cultural factors as alcohol and drug use prior to birth, neurological impairment, early neglect, abuse, physical trauma or having had multiple caregivers in early infancy. This suggests that our parenting priorities should be focused on infancy and early childhood and on an understanding of the bonding process. It is easy to see how factors surrounding the adoption experience could further intensify the emotional conflicts of early adolescence.

Parents who are aware of infant bonding and attachment are better able to prevent problems. Adoptive parents, especially, need to be aware of their children's extra vulnerabilities and concern themselves with potential attachment problems. While providing the warmth, physical comfort and love that all children require, these parents should be aware that rearing their children will require extra patience, stamina and energy. (See Appendix A)

What does all this have to say about Bethany's development during the middle school years? As Sara states, the warning signs were initially subtle and could have been interpreted as over anxiety on her part in her reactions to Bethany's symptoms. Was Bethany's behavior so different from her brother's or her peers'? Was it so striking as to be a clearly dangerous deviation from the usual early adolescent picture? It seems that as middle school progressed, Sara's worries and frustrations became more and more pronounced, and indeed Bethany's behavior became more and more disturbing.

Bethany's lack of interest in doing well, her emphasis on getting by, her choice to hang out with "bad company," her lying to avoid work and responsibility, her being, as Sara described, a "magnet for conflict," her involvement with alcohol, her gradual but steady loss of old friends and healthy activities such as art and music, her focus on action versus thought, and her distancing from her feelings were definite and important warning signs.

Academically, she also was now showing a spread in her learning scores with a low rating in the area of language expression, which probably signified a learning difficulty. It was at this point that her parents could have pursued more extensive psychoeducational testing to better understand the problems. Her grades were dropping, and she showed little interest in school, further signs of a possible formal learning disability. Since Bethany was bright and had been able to perform well in earlier grades, it took a while for the learning issues to catch up with her as the harder work of middle school progressed. That, coupled with Bethany's experiences around attachment in the first year of life, were facts pointing toward potential problems if not understood or addressed.

Sara was not wrong to note that Bethany's evasiveness, her obvious lack of knowledge about some of the assigned work, and her non-evident homework were very disturbing developments. Perhaps, they signaled a growing fear of failure, incompetence, and inability to meet the expectations of school and home. There were clues to her struggle with language in her lack of involvement in family discussions and her attempts to interrupt meaningful conversation. There was hard evidence to support the existence of language based issues in her scores which fell in the 30th percentile in language expression in formal testing.

Yet, Bethany's teachers did not support Sara's concerns. Their response could probably now be understood in light of a common tendency to see this issue as parental over involvement or the teen's behavioral issues, rather than complex learning and developmental problems. Once the school counselor referred Bethany for therapy, things became a bit better defined. There was now school recognition that a problem existed, and communication improved between the parents and the teachers. Unfortunately, the therapist suffered the same confusion as had been displayed earlier by school personnel and her previous therapist since Bethany presented herself as balanced and in control.

The outstanding signal that Bethany was heading for big trouble was the escalating conflict with peers in which she clearly was exhibiting seductive and victim-like behavior. The pattern repeated itself with her almost compulsive urge to encounter risks and repeated displays of the cigarette burns on her arms. She became torn between her fascination with danger and her need for her parents' to notice the signs of her distress. She was associating with friends whom her parents did not know and whose values were in clear conflict with theirs. That they never came to the house supported Bethany's need to keep new and questionable friends separate from her family. This stance indicated her conflict and confusion about her choices and difficulty in integrating the varying parts of her developing identity. It certainly was contrary to Sara and John's stated goals of raising their children to think and act honestly, responsibly and maturely.

The other important danger signal was Bethany's inability or unwillingness to show or talk about her worries and fears regarding any of the challenges facing her. Her denial of the traumatic experience of her oral surgery was a striking example of her tendency to avoid expressing her fears in order to present a confident facade. At the end of middle school, Bethany was still on her feet, but careening towards her high school years.

7

THE NIGHTMARE YEARS: HIGH SCHOOL

"She was destroying herself and she was also destroying the family."

By the time Bethany started high school, it was the middle of October. She was now fourteen. She felt estranged from her former friends, describing how they had abandoned her in the new school. That was hard for us to believe. More likely, we thought, she was uncomfortable because she had started school late and new alliances had been formed. However, we saw that she clearly did feel alienated and refused to join in activities with her old group. Sympathetically, we tried our best to encourage her to reestablish these friendships, but she discouraged our suggestions and began to refer to these girls as nerds, boring, not fun to be with.

Her childhood friends were involved in a variety of extra-curricular activities, but Bethany was gravitating to a new group that preferred to hang out or drive around town, windows rolled down and speakers blasting. Her new friends had no interest in organized sports or academic success. Bethany's demeanor changed completely too: her clothing, language, even her walk reflected a new identity. Bethany, who everyone thought was so bright, appeared to be sacrificing her intellect in order to fit into this new group, which provided her with excitement, a sense of risk and disdain for our values. We were dismayed when at the end of the school day, John and I began to notice bruises and hickeys on her neck and arms. When questioned she'd explain that she had bumped into a wall or a friend had given her the hickeys as a joke. Feeding into this same behavior pattern were the threatening phone calls that she began to receive at this time. Mostly, she explained, they were from girls who believed that she was trying to steal their boyfriends. How terrifying a thought that your daughter might be enjoying pain and abuse and that she was inviting this kind of behavior! We tried to talk to her about what was happening but she dismissed our concerns. We reported it all to the therapist.

Having given up her music lessons, she agreed to sign up for after school art lessons. After a short while she reverted to what had become an all too familiar pattern, frequently contriving to miss the school bus and leaving herself with no way to get to the teacher's studio. A conflict developed between her and the teacher about the same old issue; the teacher didn't think Bethany was taking her work seriously enough, and Bethany responded by calling the teacher "crazy," so by mutual agreement her lessons were discontinued. In no way did this upset Bethany. Now she could be out on the street with her friends or in the park or driving around in somebody's souped up car. While her father and I both at work fretted from a distance about her safety and choices, we were unable to maintain any control.

This was her freshman year in high school, and she was starting out on the wrong foot. Whereas she had previously confined her hostility to defying just us, she now began to cut classes and talk back to teachers and administrators when they confronted her. It made us uneasy to think that teachers and classmates would be making judgments based on her current behavior. It could impact on her entire high school career, but she didn't seem to care that she was doing so poorly. She did no homework and skipped out during tests.

As the year progressed, emergency calls would reach me at my job complaining about her behavior and telling me about her latest offense. The number of phone calls increased, and the concerns were genuine. Everyone was worried about Bethany and trying to stop this frantic escalation of negative behaviors.

Our focus began to shift. We were now down from, "I hope she gets into AP classes" to "I hope she makes it through the year." She was so negative. Any attempt at intelligent discussion about the consequences of her behavior turned into a screaming match with her shutting us completely down. Yet we couldn't avoid confronting her. Not to do so would give her the license to continue on this dangerous path.

It became so that when I was around her I could feel my insides squeezing and my heart racing as I awaited the next appalling act. She would goad me on, spitting out the car window, sneering at whatever I said, refusing to participate in family activities. There were no good conversations; everything was about her bad behavior: what she was doing, what she did do or what she might do. We kept reporting our experiences to the therapist, but Bethany didn't improve.

Here's what was scaring us. She would disappear until late at night and lie about where she had been. Phone calls would come in the middle of the night for her, only stopping when I took the phone off the hook. Her friends became more and more questionable and came from further and further away, locations where we had no connections. Each one of them had a different story—trouble with family, problems with the police, difficulties in school. At one point, we received a call from a young man who had a party at his house. Bethany had arrived with some of her friends, and when they all left, his stereo equipment left too. We lived in a constant state of heightened alert, wondering where all this had begun and where it was leading. It confounded us. Nothing in our life style could explain it, and there was nothing in her genetic background that contributed to our understanding. We wanted to blame a society whose values were so out of control, but reality showed us young people who were purposefully focused on their path to adulthood, and they were growing up in homes just like ours. Why was Bethany so out of step?

Terrified and outraged we could find no way to rein her in. I was so angry and scared all of the time it was hard to be at work and hard to be at home. I looked at every misbehaving student as if he or she was my daughter, and I was afraid I would lose my self-control with one of them. When I was offered a retirement incentive I decided to take it. I did not want to ruin a career I had loved and been proud of, and I hoped I could use the time to get Bethany on track and help Matt, who was approaching his senior year with mediocre grades, organize himself to gain acceptance into a good college.

So school ended and I retired. Bethany, because of the charity of her teachers, minimally passed all of her subjects. Remembering how the school year had begun with the two surgeries and the late start, we decided to write the year off and hope that the next one would be better. I would be home to help her with her assignments and to redirect her life, so we were hopeful.

To our dismay sophomore year got off to another horrible start. Bethany never brought any work home claiming it had been done at school, or the teacher was absent, or she was excused because she had done such a terrific job on some project, or she lost her back pack, or someone took it and hid it. There was always some new excuse. I would check up on her and call the teacher the next day. By the time the call was returned, the assignment was way past due. Sometimes we would drive back to school, find a custodian to let us in, get her books from her locker, if they were there, and return home only to find out that she had not copied down the assignment. I was exhausting myself trying to jump over all of the hurdles she set up.

At the dinner table, she appeared to be having trouble following conversations and would explode if we told her to help with dinner preparation or cleanup. When I did get the opportunity to see her school work, I would find that she copied other students' homework, errors and all, and often handed in her brother's

earlier assignments taken off our computer but remarkably unnoted by her teachers who must have known some of what was going on. Bethany continued
attending therapy, and we continued to voice our concerns about possible drug
and alcohol use, but when she was tested the results were negative. In our ignorance, we had taken her for several random urine tests, but did not understand
their limitations and did not know about the more reliable hair follicle test.

Anxious to stop the downward spiral and to provide her opportunities for success, we again encouraged her to become more involved in school activities and
get a job. We needed to help her impose more structure on her life and hoped
that through this she would develop some positive goals. She joined the soccer
team and was able to get an after school job. For a short while the arrangement
seemed to work for her, and we had a brief respite. But her success was short
lived.

By the second term of her sophomore year, she was again cutting classes, skip-
ping soccer practice and her job, staying out late, and failing every subject. She
got into fights with teachers and administrators at school. She was so absorbed
with her social life she barely had time to eat. When she did come home, she
refused to communicate with us, and if we would say something she would cut us
off with one of her two favorite responses: "Whatever!" or "Blah, blah, blah, blah,
blah!"

As the year went on she stopped coming home after school. Our house was the
last stop on the bus route so it was often quite late by the time that I realized she
had missed the bus. By then, she was nowhere to be found. When I tried to circumvent this problem by picking her up at school at the end of the day, I found
that she had cut out early, and I didn't have a clue as to where to find her. Her
friends would lie about her whereabouts and cover up for her, and I felt that they
were laughing at me as I drove away on a futile search.

I was now, like Bethany, constantly on the go. I worked out a system with the
school whereby they would call me anytime if she left without permission, and I
would begin a search around town for her. I would go into her friends' homes
that had been left unlocked and check out local stores in a constant quest to track
her down. Often missing the school bus in the morning because she couldn't get
up on time, she would get out of my car at the school's front door, and then I
would watch her sneak out the back so that she could go to her boyfriend's house.
I'd pick her up and redeposit her only to see the process occur all over again.
Bethany, embarrassed by my constant presence, called me the "Mommy stalker."

Each night I would get in bed and lie there trying to figure out new strategies,
a better way to tell her how worried we were. I tried to find the words to show her

what the consequences for this behavior were, but it all fell on deaf ears. Well meaning friends and relatives told us about teenage rebellion and minimized our concerns by recalling their own misconduct in their youth. This only heightened our sense of hopelessness.

As the days passed, Bethany appeared angrier and angrier. We never knew what mood to expect. She was a tyrant. Our family life revolved around her. While protesting that she didn't want to be the center of attention, she manipulated her life and ours so that she was the center of attention. Every conversation dealt with her and what she had or hadn't done that day. Often she pretended not to hear what was being said. When it was repeated, it gave her time to conceive another lie, and then she found a way to change the subject, diverting attention from herself and often starting an argument between John and me. We were frantic and dreaded the persistent ringing of the phone. Frequently, it meant another school suspension or required another meeting which would accomplish nothing more than hearing her empty promises to reform. We felt her actions were reflecting drug usage, but we had no solid evidence to back this up. With all of the garbage in her room there was nothing that we recognized as drug residue or equipment and her drug tests still were negative.

She was now regularly stealing money and jewelry from us and, in response, we began locking bedroom doors and hiding our valuables. One summer weekend, we went out of town for a wedding. We were only going to be gone for the day. We left Bethany with clear instructions and made arrangements for her to spend the time at a friend's house, returning only to care for the pets. We thought we had covered our bases. Nevertheless, we returned home to find the remains of dead frogs smashed against rocks near our swimming pool, the corpses a gift from her friends. Our dog was reeling from the effects of beer and alcohol, and Bethany was nowhere to be found.

We were horrified at the cruelty shown by her friends, her inability to stop them, and her attraction to these characters. Again friends tried to reassure us that all teenagers did outrageous things. Not placated, we became prisoners in our own home, afraid to leave the house for fear that she would steal from us or have her friends over who would defile our home or cause some other mayhem.

Caring relatives all spoke to Bethany who would passively respond, "I'll try to behave." Reassured, they reported the success of their conversations to us, but nothing changed. Well-meaning friends, when questioning her, heard how demanding we were and how well she was really doing in school. They told us we needed to ease up on her. On our part, we felt all the negation of our feelings, but we could not bring ourselves to share the full truth about Bethany. Each day brought a new outrageous behavior on her part, increasing the tension among the rest of us. No one knew how to react to the wildness, so we each compensated in our own way. Matthew withdrew into himself, staying in his room until dinner and then quickly returning there when done with his meal. I tiptoed around, holding my breath and trying to be pleasant and entertaining in order to lighten the mood, and John just got more irate trying to impose sane rules on this insane fury. In the meantime, a friend commiserated with me and told me how Bethany was persona non grata in town. Other mothers didn't want their children around her.

We were not passive in our responses. We had taken her for drug tests—all negative. We had tried all of the standard strategies—rewards for good behavior, groundings for breaking the rules, sports, jobs, and therapy, but we were reactive. We would do something in response to one of her actions, but she was calling the shots. Nothing worked. We were not in control. She would jump out of her bedroom window and meet a boyfriend at a prearranged place. Sometimes we had no idea where she was going. Other times, she would be hanging out with strange young men only to return home looking exhausted and bruised.

The national news at the time focused on a mother who had handcuffed her uncontrollable teenager to her bed in order to keep her at home. I understood how she had arrived at that decision as John and I argued about how to ground Bethany.

A walk into Bethany's room screamed that it harbored some disintegrating soul. Her room was piled high with dirty laundry, cigarette butts, CDs, papers, half empty food containers, balls of hair, all kinds of debris, our missing clothing, and stolen items from a variety of stores. We were tempted to report the thievery to the police, but were stopped by the fear that their response would damage her even more.

When she would spit out the car window or talk about her future as a truck driver, I would silently ask myself, "Is this my child?" I had always believed that children reflected their parents' attitudes and behaviors, but where were we here? And where was she? Where was the Bethany who had loved music, art, sports, animals and life?

By now, Bethany had a new boyfriend. She would spend all her time driving around with him or hanging out in his house. She went there during school and stayed until late at night when she would call us to pick her up. He never came to our house and if we happened to pick up the phone when he called he would hang up, but we knew who it was. Frequently, she would return from a day with him with black and blue marks on her arms. There was always some ridiculous explanation for these wounds, but we believed that he was mistreating her. She would call us at 12:30 or 1:00 in the morning to pick her up, and it was only then that I would get to speak to her because she had long since stopped coming home for meals.

On one occasion when I picked her up, I asked her how her day had been, and she proceeded to describe what she perceived as a typical day at school. I knew it was a lie as I had gotten a call earlier in the day reporting her absence and I went berserk. I started smacking her, flailing wildly, as I drove the car, crying and screaming simultaneously. It was just the weapon she wanted because now she could tell all of her friends that her mother hit her.

She was destroying herself, and she was also destroying the family. I was in a constant rage, and John and I could barely be civil to each other. We argued about what had caused all of this and how we should or shouldn't handle it. Bethany was a master at manipulating us. She often refused to recognize her father or talk to him. She played on my sympathies constantly, complaining about his attitude towards her and trying to drive a wedge between the two of us. Dinners when we did manage a meal together would disintegrate into screaming matches between John and me while Bethany would retreat to get away from "all of your craziness."

John and I decided to take another approach. Since we couldn't redirect her from within the family, we went to the school and requested an evaluation. If they recognized that she had a classifiable problem, we reasoned, we would have an ally in our quest to refocus her. Our appeal was to be based on the argument that because Bethany was having serious trouble in school and was in danger of failing the entire year, she might have an undiagnosed learning problem that had only begun to show itself now that she was of an age when school demanded more intense work. Perhaps the work was too difficult for her, and this was her way of escaping.

The evaluation was done over three days. On the first day, the examiner noted that Bethany was cooperative and agreeable, but this good attitude quickly dissipated. By the second day, her behavior became distracted, her attendance became erratic, and she was making excuses for her unavailability. As the report said, "She was not overtly defiant, but was passively resistant."

By the end of the time allotted, the tester made the decision "to prioritize the order of testing to include some projectives," this in response to "her waning spirit of cooperation." The examiner found her resistant to giving up any of her anger toward her parents and terrified of revealing any of her inner feelings and secrets. Bethany "admitted to being extremely sensitive and vulnerable, using very rigid defenses to guard against further emotional pain." Her achievement tests indicated similar results to earlier testing, above grade level scores in math skills and scattered results in the varied reading parts of the test.

As for her emotional functioning, Bethany "presents as a very lonely, fearful, anxious and depressed young lady with a poor self-image." The examiner went on to describe a child whose "nurturance and care appear to be unfulfilled," who "needs her mommy, but has ambivalent feelings towards her" and who "feels intense, but unexplained hostility toward her father." In order to "protect herself from intense emotional pain, she withdraws from close interpersonal relationships especially with females," and she has both "impulsive and compulsive tendencies." Her "response to her dilemma is to hold on to her anger and negativism and to behave in a self-punitive manner."

Conclusion—no learning disability. Bethany's "intellectual capacity is well above average and her academic difficulties are due to emotional factors." She is a "little girl whose dependency needs have been thwarted and who consequently feels rejected." What they would offer her was "supportive assistance as a non-classified resource student to cope with her current emotional turmoil."

As I write this now, I see that the rejection Bethany was feeling was from all of her mothers, something she had not been able to absorb. The years of therapy, the discussions of adoption, the story books, and the many steps we had taken to make her comfortable with her life story had been unavailing, and now it had festered into this huge boil that was destroying her. Whether this self-destruction took the form of depression or anger, reckless behavior, withdrawal or aggression, it stemmed from her intense feeling of abandonment and her inability to communicate this to the people who loved her and cared about her.

Bethany was assigned to the Resource Room for academic support. We had a strong suspicion that this support would not be effective, but as a teacher I knew the routine. The school would make the most benign recommendation, and we would cooperate until we exhausted all of their programs. Then we would come in with our own plan. As expected, nothing changed. She rarely went for the extra help. "It's boring. They treat me like an idiot. I don't need it." But she continued to fail her classes and cut school. The school was as frustrated as we were.

Bethany had a big test coming up. She was supposed to be studying in her room, but she came downstairs and announced that she had to go out to meet someone. "It's important. Jenny left something at Bill's house, and I have to get it for her."

"Why can't Jenny get it herself?" I asked, ignoring the fact that I had no idea who Jenny was.

"Bill's mother won't let Jenny in the house, so I have to get it," she replied.

I knew Bethany was lying again. She had no intention of studying for the test or taking it. It was obvious she had made her plans and needed an excuse to get out of the house.

I told her, "If you leave now don't plan on coming back. Go stay with one of your friends who cares so much about your well being." What else could I do? I was just formalizing what was apparent anyway; she wasn't really living at home. Late at night she called. "Ma! I have nowhere to go. I'm in the middle of town, and no one is here."

"Where are your friends?" I asked

"They're all home. I can't go to their houses."

"I'll find you a place to go," I told her. "Wait there."

What I did was call all of the hospitals that had psychiatric centers for teenagers. I needed to get her some serious help and us a reprieve from the daily turmoil. We picked her up and drove her to one of them. A young intern on duty interviewed all of us, separately and together. When finished with Bethany he called us in, told us that this was normal "teenage behavior" and that we needed to "get a grip." I wanted to strangle him, but I settled for alternating between crying and laughing, clearly not able to "get a grip."

We discussed what happened with her therapist. He too was acknowledging defeat, having no understanding of what was really happening. On the one hand, Bethany would show up fairly regularly for her appointments, but she continued to deny that she was using drugs. On the other hand, he knew her disreputable friends and though he continued to listen to her, he believed that most of her talk was meaningless drivel. He had spent years talking with her about all of the usual subjects in an effort to find the causes for this behavior.

In addition to drugs and friends, they had explored the possibility of learning problems, destructive family behaviors, depression, lack of goals. He was baffled and like us, felt he had reached the limits of his ability to help her. Rarely did they explore the subject of adoption or the possibility of attachment disorder. It seemed too far-fetched an explanation. Panicked we begged him to continue her therapy until we could devise another plan. At least this was an hour a week of organized structured time with an adult whom we trusted. He agreed.

As our next step, the therapist suggested that perhaps he had been misreading Bethany. "Maybe she's depressed and would benefit from medication." An appointment was made for an evaluation by a psychiatrist. A separate interview for each of us consisted of the reading of a checklist describing a variety of behaviors and a brief interview with the patient. After about twenty minutes, we were sent on our way, Bethany holding a prescription for Prozac and none of us any more knowledgeable about what her problems were. Bethany took the prescription and crumbled it up. "I'm not putting that stuff in my body," she announced.

All these maneuvers were getting us nowhere. Bethany's life continued as before. She was wildly out of control and would accept no responsibility. Finally, the therapist offered to help with an intervention, and a meeting was arranged among all of us. Bethany, when confronted with our list of concerns, reluctantly agreed to go to a hospital for treatment. I believe her compliance was her acknowledgement that something had to be done, that she was miserable and just couldn't control herself.

It was impossible to convince our insurance company to pay for residential treatment. After all, she had been in therapy, she had no proven drug problems, and she did not appear to be what they considered a danger to herself or to others. After living through her destructive behaviors, I couldn't imagine what would qualify for "danger to herself," but we could not win the point. We did, however, persuade them to pay for day treatment at the hospital. There they had a program for children with Oppositional Defiant Disorder, a catch-all phrase for these kinds of behaviors. She was scheduled to begin immediately after the school term ended.

The end of her sophomore year arrived. Her report card came; her highest mark was a sixteen. The others were all zeroes. It couldn't be any worse.

Matt was preparing to graduate from high school, and I began to develop renewed hope. Perhaps when he was away at college she would feel less competition from him. Bethany complained that Matthew was "always so perfect." Perhaps this time alone with her could help us to repair our relationships and get her back on track. Maybe the day treatment wouldn't even be necessary. We tried to make a plan with her: get a job for the summer, go to summer school, get your life on track. She agreed.

Graduation day arrived for Matt. We dropped Bethany off at work and arranged to pick her up for the graduation ceremony, a big event for Matthew as he was scheduled to win several commendations for academic improvement and community service. Family traveled from out of state to celebrate the day with us. We arrived at her workplace and waited outside for a while, but she never appeared. I went in only to find out that when she arrived she told her boss that she had to quit the job because of personal family problems and then had immediately left. I returned to the cars to try to explain to her grandmother, uncles, aunts, and cousins what had just transpired.

The day was ruined for Matthew, for all of us. A day of celebration turned into a day of mourning with everybody's concern being for Bethany's absence. Bethany did not show up for the graduation, for the dinner party, or for the next three days. She had never been away for so long before, and we were distraught.

For the first time, but not the last, we called the police and provided a photo with her description and a list of her friends and their phone numbers. The officers were not very encouraging and talked a lot about the epidemic of out of control teenagers in affluent suburban communities. It did not appear that they would conduct an active search, but rather would hold the photograph "in case something turned up." The words were chilling.

It was Matthew who found out through the teenage grapevine where she was. She had been staying nearby at her friend Abby's house. John drove there to pick her up and bring her home. It was bad timing because she was in the company of her friends when he arrived, and with their silent but belligerent support, she refused to accompany him.

Abby's parents were also present. Instead of seeing them as our allies, we viewed them as part of the problem. Why hadn't Abby's parents called us in all this time to at least tell us that Bethany was safe? Did Abby's parents know that we had no idea where our daughter was for three days? Were they being fed the same lies by Bethany and Abby that we were? Did they think they were supporting Bethany by helping her to miss her brother's graduation, her relatives' visit, and worrying us sick for three days not knowing where Bethany was?

What awful stories had Bethany told them about us, and if she had told them that she was being abused, why hadn't they called the police? Abby's parents were not going to help us get Bethany home, so John returned home at a loss about what to do.

Again, I called the police this time for help in getting her home. They came to our house and then drove me back to Abby's but, of course, the kids had already left. We drove around until we found them in a local park, and Bethany was told that it was time to come home.

When she returned home, she was sullen and argumentative, but compliant. The police officer told us that they could not keep coming to our house, that we ought to get help controlling her. He gave us the name of the local Youth Officer who could talk to her. Calls there were not returned. We called the local Mental Health Association who offered us the names of several support groups, two of which I attended a couple of times. There I encountered the parents of young criminals. We had not reached that point.

I called Family Court where I was offered information about a PINS petition (Persons In Need of Supervision), a legal procedure for parents and guardians to get help with runaway and incorrigible teenagers, but Bethany was fast approaching her sixteenth birthday and this route would no longer be available to us.

When her birthday came, Bethany demanded a driver's permit, but we refused to cooperate. After all, we told her, "If you cannot act maturely enough to get to school and do what needs to be done, how responsible will you be behind the wheel of a car?" Her response was like the little girl with the matches. When we left the house, she took the spare set of keys to the second car and took off without even a permit and without our permission.

Again, Bethany disappeared. We called her boyfriend to ask if he knew where she was. We explained that we didn't want to call the police, but if we did we would report a stolen car. He denied any knowledge, but we soon found the car parked and abandoned not far from our house. Bethany was gone, but we were reluctant to call the police after our last contact with them. Instead we called every one of her friends and all of the names that she had scribbled on bits of paper that were tossed in her trash collection. Finally, after several days, she returned home with no explanation except that she needed one last fling before she began the program at the hospital. It was as though she felt entitled to "go crazy" before beginning the program that she was scheduled to start the next day. But she was also clearly saying, "I'm in charge here. You can't tell me what I can and can't do."

While waiting for Bethany to enter the program at the hospital, I had put together a social history of Bethany's life starting from when she had joined our family. I repeated what we had been told by her foster mother about how bright and alert she was. I talked about her many talents, precocious behaviors, and leadership abilities. I also described her unwillingness to set goals, the conflicts in school, troubled relationships and rebellious and reckless behaviors. I wanted to make it easier for the new therapists to get a complete picture of her and the family, and to see what we had already tried in our attempts to help her mature into a well rounded adult. I also wanted to avoid answering the same questions that were repeated each time she started with a new therapist or new program.

Bethany began the new schedule. I drove twenty miles back and forth, twice a day, five days a week. She still had her nights and her weekends to reconnect with her buddies. At the program, she met more teenagers from similar backgrounds with similar problems. They were youngsters who abused drugs, cut school, and stole from their families. Some were suicidal and some had problems on the Internet, but most had not escalated into serious criminal behaviors. A few of the children were adopted; most were not. The subject, if it came up, was glanced over as it was not a common thread. However, logic does tell us that a usual symptom can have many causes. Again, an opportunity to discover attachment problems was lost.

Every Friday, the hospital called the insurance company to have Bethany recertified, and on the same day they did a urine analysis, being no smarter about the hair follicle test than we had been, to check that she was drug free. Once a week we met as a family with a therapist, and once a week we met with other similar families.

In the beginning, Bethany was cooperative and even appeared to enjoy the program. She was making new friends easily. She was taking one course in their summer school to make up for one of her failures; she was participating in a variety of groups; she was substance free, and she was adhering to a curfew that we had imposed on her. Although she kept reasonable hours and was compliant in the program, there were already undercurrents of trouble. She still never spent time at home engaged with the family. She was out every night or buried in front of the TV. John and I held our breath hoping that her behavior would turn around, and she would benefit from the hospital therapy. She didn't. At the end of her first week, she failed to come home one night. The next day when she returned she was very contrite. She knew she shouldn't have broken curfew, but she just couldn't help herself. The event was discussed individually, in family groups, and in patient groups, but we were all playing our customary roles. Bethany was contrite; we were angry; the outsiders were surprised. It was a dance, performed without emotion, and at the end of six weeks when she was discharged, she disappeared again.

This time Bethany went down to the Jersey shore with a bunch of boys and called us at 3:00 AM to tell us where she was. Her original plan had been to come home early from town that evening and go the next night with her brother and some friends to a concert. When it got late and it was apparent that she wasn't coming home, John and I went up to her room to look for clues to her whereabouts. Among the things that we found were spent matches on the flat roof outside her bedroom window which meant that she had been either carelessly smoking or lighting fires, endangering all of our lives. Two days later she returned having missed the concert, disappointing her brother and friends, and getting into a fight on the phone with her boyfriend who was understandably angry that she had spent three days with other boys. And that was not the end of it.

When she got off the phone her father told her to pick up the matches. She said she would do it later and he said, "No, you'll do it now!" It escalated to her usual "F you!" and his marching her forcefully over to the steps and telling her to "Go upstairs and get rid of the matches now!" She was screaming hysterically, "You're gonna' kill me! I hate you! You're not my father!"

Somehow, it ended. I had been in the bathroom probably avoiding the scene, but when I came out she had apparently beeped a male friend and was soon picked up only to disappear again, telling us nothing about her plans.

This time we decided to try another tactic. We would make no phone calls; we would not try to track her down. On the fourth night she called at about 12:30. She was crying and asked why I hadn't called her. "I didn't know where you were."

"Yes, you did."

"No, I didn't. Were you at Abby's?"

"No."

"Then I didn't know where you were."

She told me how much she missed me and asked if John was home. "If he's home, I'm not coming home," she declared. There it was. She was telling me to make a choice. I avoided her demand and we decided to meet the next day to talk.

After the small talk, in an attempt to shake her up and force her to come to her senses, I told her that we did not want her back in the house if we were just going to repeat our past patterns, and I offered her some options. She could return home, follow our rules and go back to the local high school, or we could try to find an affordable boarding school that would accept her, but she would probably have to repeat at least one year of school, or we could hand her over to the Department of Social Services and have them place her in a residential setting, or she could make her own arrangements asking someone else to assume legal custody.

These choices probably sound like I was a rational person, thinking clearly and offering a reasonable plan, but nothing could be further from the truth. These were not really choices at all. Why would she ever choose to place herself in the custody of Social Services or to be sent to a school where they would put her back a year? Who else would want to assume legal custody of this troubled child? I appeared to be thinking clearly, but I really wasn't. I offered her those choices, futilely hoping she would admit her mistakes and change her behaviors, but I knew it was useless. As I awaited her next act of rebellion, tears were always just at the surface. I was functioning with little sleep and no peace. Up all night, I listened for the phone, watched for car lights, tuned in to late night news in a constant state of hypervigilance, as I painfully came to the realization that none of the dreams I had for my daughter was going to be realized.

When I returned home from our meeting, John discovered that a small pouch containing money for tolls that we kept in the car was missing. I was furious at myself and her. Why did I keep letting her use me in that way? All the talking and apologizing and promises to reform had been just another ruse, and I was left with feelings of rage and stupidity. Would it always go on with her playing me like this? Did she have any sense of conscience? She seemed to be moving even further away, but despite this last act and everything else, Bethany chose to return home. Again she apologized, this time for giving into temptation with her petty theft. She didn't know why she did these things; she wanted to live at home in a normal family, and she wanted to finish her education, she said.

I set up an appointment with the school principal to see how she could pull her education together. The meeting was very positive. He explained how she could still graduate high school in four years if she was willing to go to school in the summer to make up for failed courses. As a former teacher, I imagined I knew that at least a few of her teachers must be grumbling about the apparent lack of consequences for her disobedience and disrespect. She wasn't even asked to apologize. As a parent, I was extremely grateful that she could move on, but I was also somewhat ambivalent. We seemed to be the only ones who thought she should be accountable for her actions, but it didn't matter because the plan quickly fell apart, and it was soon more of the same.

During this time, we were following up on the therapy plan that had been devised for us when we were at the hospital. We were to go to a satellite therapy center twice a week, once for individual therapy and once a week for family therapy. Once a month we were scheduled for group therapy with other equally challenged families.

We started our first session with a general discussion while I gave the therapist Bethany's social history, newly updated from the last submission. We spent the weeks going over the familiar discussions about behavior, goals, relationships, school, as they say, "same old, same old." Again, Bethany amiably told the therapist how well she was doing in all aspects of school. Our apprehensions earned us suggestions about our negativity and lack of sense of humor. For a while, we again questioned our own sanity.

That year promised to be another one from hell. At about this time, we got a call from the boyfriend's parents. They wanted to help us straighten out our relationship as clearly Bethany was upset by it all, and the family violence she was reporting to them couldn't continue. Poor Bethany was so unhappy, and they really wanted to help. Never mind that we suspected that their son was providing Bethany with drugs, hideaways from school, bruises on her body. They thought we needed their help in straightening all of this out and in understanding this new generation. I was steaming! Their misconceptions were insulting and almost intolerable, but for some reason I kept my mouth shut, not divulging what I knew about their son and understanding that they, too, were just trying to help Bethany. But Bethany was long past any help now.

She stayed out late at night, slept all day, never went to school, wouldn't talk to us. Meanwhile, I threatened to stand naked in the center of town to embarrass her in front of her friends, trying to get her to change her outrageous behavior. Like the Ancient Mariner, I stopped everyone I knew to tell them about my daughter's latest misdeeds, begging for help. I, too, was out of control.

In our driveway were the EMS and two patrol cars. Neighbors drove by and slowed as they passed the house to see what was going on. John had called 911 after I had complained that I was having trouble breathing. It was the day after the call from the credit card company, right after Bethany and I had gotten into another screaming battle about her behavior, and she had cursed at me and told me to "stop ruining her life." I started to hyperventilate, gasping for breath, trying to calm myself down. John feared I was having a heart attack and there we were, our disintegrating lives on parade for the world to see. Bethany ran out of the house in fear and in shame while fifteen strangers with oxygen masks and pressure cuffs, two-way radios, legal pads, and forms ran into our kitchen wondering what kind of family we were.

That moment was like an epiphany for me. The pundits, the teachers, the psychologists, had told us that Bethany had to hit bottom before she could be helped. But like us, Bethany did not know where her bottom was, and she certainly didn't have the control to make the necessary changes in her attitude, her friends, her behaviors, and her goals. But I had to give credit where it was due, and those experts were partly right. Someone had to reach the bottom, and I was that someone.

My bottom came when I saw those strangers standing in my kitchen, watching me breathe into a paper bag to stop the hyperventilation. Right then I made myself a promise. I would seek help to regain control of my life even if it meant that Bethany had to leave the house so that the rest of our family could be saved. Reluctantly, I acknowledged that Bethany would have to endure her third separation in order for all of us to survive.

Early Monday morning, I made two phone calls: one to a therapist for myself to help in taking back that control and the second to the school to request a meeting with the Committee on Special Education to review her educational plan which was clearly not working. We would need the school's cooperation in finding and paying for an effective residential program for Bethany, and we would have to go through a slow process to convince the state that this was the only viable solution to Bethany's problems.

The first step towards that goal would be a meeting with the committee to make our case that Resource Room assistance was not working. This was not hard to prove since Bethany's marks had not improved nor had her attendance. Clearly, she needed more than this approach could offer.

During the meeting her evaluation was produced as part of the discussion. The psychologist referred to the examiner's comments that Bethany "displayed a great deal of hostility towards her parents, especially towards her mother, who was a teacher, and who Bethany felt made unreasonable demands on her school performance." By this time, I was numb. Was it unreasonable to expect her to get up and go to school? Do homework? Take and pass tests? They also had a copy of the psychiatric assessment from the hospital. Mood disorder and Oppositional Defiant Disorder it concluded.

We got what we needed, and Bethany was finally classified as emotionally handicapped, and a recommendation was made for a school that had a program appropriate for her needs. We were given two programs to look at. The first was a vocationally focused morning program that Bethany immediately rejected. Bethany thought she would be bored and stigmatized by the setting. The second, the one she chose, a self-contained program for gifted, but handicapped youngsters in one of the other high schools in our county. She never gave it a chance. She went for two days. After that she hung out in the cafeteria for a week, cooperatively distributing marijuana for a new friend she had met on the first day, and finally she stopped going all together.

By now, we decided to just let it happen. We no longer tried to wake her up in the morning or to keep her home at night. Our only response to her was to tell her that this couldn't go on forever, that eventually there would be a price to pay, and that right now we did not know what that price would be. We were not threatening her; we were just being realistic.

Meanwhile, we went back to the Committee on Special Education in our school district. At the end of a very long meeting we won our point. Bethany was approved for residential schooling, and we were advised to look at the schools on the state's approved list. We selected three to preview. One was a lockup for youthful offenders; it was very punitive. One was a lockup in a mental hospital; all of the children were heavily medicated, and one was for children who had severe learning disabilities. None of them fit the bill, and I reported back to the committee that I intended to look elsewhere.

While Bethany persisted in her dangerous lifestyle, I single-mindedly continued on my quest to find her an appropriate school and refused to engage in any arguments with her. Instead I resorted to her favorite "whatever" as my frequent response.

Bethany was thrown off balance by my new behavior and stayed closer to home, apparently now nervous about the constancy of my love. But she did not make any attempt to get back into school or alter her friendships. So I stood firm in my commitment to find the right program and save her life.

It looked like our only hope was going to be a regular boarding school which we really couldn't afford. In the meantime, I talked to everyone I knew, hoping to find information about residential programs for her.

It was on a visit to my old school where I finally found the help we needed. Everyone there knew about Bethany and her problems. They all remembered her when she had been younger and still full of potential. When the special education supervisor overheard me talking, she broke into the conversation and sent me on a path to the school that would help Bethany turn her life around. And it was my therapist who put me in touch with an education attorney who helped me find the legal precedent that would get our school district to pay the tuition at the school we finally chose.

John and I went for our interview at the new school. The Admissions Director didn't even want to talk to Bethany. Dealing with other kids like Bethany, she knew that would be pointless. She was actually most interested in whether we could go along with the program that would separate Bethany and us completely for the first eight weeks, and after that the contacts would be tightly controlled. During the interview, the Admissions Director did not try to minimize our experiences by talking about teenage stages and hysterical parents. She believed what we told her.

I tried to tell Bethany about the school, its dress code, restrictions on radios, phone calls, twelve step program etc. I told her about the kids we had met there, but she wouldn't pay attention. "Whatever!" she replied. She didn't listen, but she didn't fight us either. It was as though she knew this step was inevitable and could possibly take the choices of daily life out of her hands for now, something she needed very badly.

What was there about this school that was so effective when all of our attempts at reining this child in had been so futile? The Admissions Director summed it up, "We have complete control over these kids for twenty-four hours a day.

There are no outside influences. We are fifteen miles from the nearest town. We control what these kids wear, who they talk to and what they hear, and what they say. They are away from alcohol and drugs, TV, radio, low life friends, and enabling relatives. We isolate them from you until we believe that they will not be able to coax you into giving them what they think they need. They do their schoolwork here because if they don't they will be deprived of the things that are really important like contact with their family. And we do it with your blessings because you have tried everything else, and it didn't work, did it? We reorder their priorities and get them to see what is really important."

The night before she was to leave for her new school, we let her stay out, knowing that she would be exhausted the next day and would sleep on the long car ride. We had been warned and seen on an earlier visit that many youngsters try to run away and need to be brought to the school by hired escorts. But as exhausted as we were, Bethany was equally worn out. Her years of doing battle had taken its toll on her, too. Her face was drawn, and she was clearly underweight. We didn't think she had much fight left in her and was looking to us to figure out how to stop her. Reluctantly, we drove her to the school.

Back when Bethany was a baby and we first brought her home from her foster home, we were so filled with elation and gratitude for our good fortune in having Matthew's biological sister added to our family. We could never have envisioned the day when we would be forced to send her away. Now, we prayed that this was what would bring us back our hopes and dreams, our adorable little girl whom we loved so much.

As we drove up that mud road in the Catskill Mountains on our way to the school, past the farm with its ramshackle outbuildings and the grazing cows, Bethany woke up to look around incredulously, "What are you people thinking?" she asked.

"Someday when this is all over, I'll write a book and tell you what I was thinking," I responded. "And perhaps, you'll keep a journal and be able to tell me what you were thinking, too!"

◆   ◆   ◆

As described in the previous chapter, adolescence is normally a stressful and troubled time of life. We are told in the book *Normal Adolescence* (1968) compiled by the Committee on Adolescence that this stage is marked by radical changes in three major areas of development: physical, psychological, and cultural. The onset of adolescence begins with the hormonal changes taking place in puberty, which for girls is usually between the ages of ten to thirteen and for boys between twelve to sixteen. The process of puberty itself is anywhere between one to five years duration.

During this time, the adolescent often experiences overwhelming fatigue, an increase in physical activity, a need for relief from tension, and an increased intensity of eating and sleeping habits. Puberty brings marked changes in the organs involved in sex and reproduction. The young person experiences a preoccupation with the timing of menstruation and the size of the penis and breasts. For young people at this stage of development, this period can be marked by involuntary and embarrassing body reactions and a heightened sense of self-consciousness.

Along with these significantly important physiological changes in puberty, there are critical changes taking place psychologically as well. Such factors as height, obesity, acne and masturbation can cause intense anxiety, and the child often experiences guilt over sexual thoughts. The changing body creates overstimulating ideas and feelings which generally threaten the adolescent's emotional balance.

Because the adolescent is in the passageway between childhood and adulthood, she is compelled culturally to rebel against the rules and values of society in order to grow and mature. All adolescents are particularly vulnerable to the strain of these rapid and striking changes taking place physically and psychologically and the demands made upon them by this stage of life to take a position on what they feel is important sociologically, what they are willing to stand for.

Every culture has a set of universal rules, laws, and customs, and its own criteria for what defines reaching adulthood. In our society, adolescence is a separate time marked by intense and exclusive allegiance to the peer group, while adult mores and cultural institutions are challenged. The adolescent has the job of observing culture in order to assess the climate for ethical behavior. What she may see in our current culture is that success and respectability often do not include making ethical choices, and often there do not seem to be consequences for unethical behavior. Indeed, it appears these unethical behaviors are often rewarded.

The child has to determine for herself if society is living by its own stated moral standards. There are many examples of the conflict between the explicit standards and those that the child sees carried out around her every day. Her personal choices can only be understood through an awareness of the culture in which those choices are being made. These choices indicate the level of her rebellion against parental and societal expectations.

Along with the cultural influences on the adolescent's choices, other elements impact her progress towards maturity. These include the underlying conditions created by genetics and the life experiences that influence her psychological development and which undoubtedly have not yet been resolved. Such resolution would not be developmentally possible or even desirable at such a young age.

For all adolescents, there is the struggle between dependence on the parent and a wish for independence. This struggle will go on in various stages for many years before it is possible to reach a resolution. In the meantime, there are two major stages to the adolescent period. The earlier stage includes an increase in sexual and aggressive urges which abates somewhat in the mid-teens and the later phase which reflects developing mastery as the adolescent becomes increasingly regulated and reliable. When some equilibrium is finally achieved, the end of adolescence is signaled.

As the child moves from early to late adolescence, adults start to expect her to assume more mature roles in society. While some teenagers strive to succeed at every point during this consolidation, others respond with an overwhelming rejection of social expectations. Both the conforming and non-conforming respond to the same set of social realities, one by joining the establishment and the other by rejecting it. Within these two major groups, there are a number of subgroups. The philosophical stance in each grouping can usually be identified by the manner of dress, the type of music listened to, the activities engaged in, and the typical form of speech that is used. The adolescent almost always finds others like herself and associates exclusively with the group that most closely matches her philosophy, view of the world, and internal psychological self.

All adolescents have to practice being adults before the behavior becomes more reliable. In general, they do not want to be conformists; they want to be recognized as individuals. While this process is playing out, parents are afraid of the consequences of impulsive or aggressive behavior that many adolescents do not seem to be bothered by, such as dropping out of school, drug and alcohol use, pregnancy, automobile accidents, and even death. Indeed, the impulsivity of adolescence often results in accidents, the major cause of death in ages fifteen to nineteen.

The adults in these young people's lives are often highly stressed and anxious, both in the presence of the adolescent and under the influence of the power the adolescent exerts upon the environment. The adults are often critical and angry and frequently cannot view this stage of development as having constructive elements; neither do they seem to be able to call upon their own experiences during adolescence to help them understand the current generation.

Frequently, there is ambivalence on the part of parents regarding the use of an automobile, an obvious symbol of autonomy for the developing adolescent. While driving presents undeniable dangers to the adolescent and others on the road, there are many advantages as well. The ability to drive helps the teenager work out issues of independence from parents and adult supervision, while it affords self-sufficiency and privacy. Teenagers view their use of a car as a sign of entry into adulthood.

All in all, the majority of young people make an adjustment to moving through adolescence, which results in developing abilities, entering an occupation, choosing a mate, having children, and making a commitment to the community. Achieving adulthood should bring a positive resolution to this developmental stage and should include the following:

- Separation and independence from parents
- Attainment of a sexual identity
- Development of a work ethic
- Development of ethical and moral values
- Ability to develop lasting relationships and enter into sexual love
- Establishment of an adult relationship with parents.

With the successful resolution of a relatively average or normal adolescent passage in mind, we turn to Harold S. Koplewicz, M.D. in his book *It's Nobody's Fault* (1996) to help us understand what happens when something goes wrong and development goes off track, creating serious pain and anxiety for the adolescent involved and for her bewildered parents.

According to the 2000 U.S. census figures, 28.6 percent of the population is under the age of twenty. At least 12 percent of those adolescents, or about 9.6 million, come into the world with severe imbalances in their brain chemistry. Parents of these adolescents often get the impression from those around them that they are at fault for their child's difficulties, while, in reality, a child's brain chemistry is not the fault of her parents, or of anyone.

Conditions that exist in brain development are there because of how the brain works, not what parents the do. The medical reality is that in the process of conception there is what Dr. Koplewicz calls "DNA roulette," which can create a "no-fault brain disorder." The picture can be further complicated in adolescence due to normally changing brain chemistry, which necessarily brings insecurity and instability. Indeed, research is now showing us that brain disorders, along with the difficulties that accompany them are as unavoidable and out of our control as any other genetic condition, such as diabetes or epilepsy.

It is valuable for parents to learn a bit about brain chemistry in order to understand what their children experience. The brain is organized around a system of networks that transmits messages from one part of the brain to another. The chemicals transmitting these messages are called neurotransmitters. If they malfunction, problems result in the neurological system, sending messages that are too weak, too strong, blocked or misdirected.

Although there are many important neurotransmitters, three have been carefully studied for the purposes of childhood psychiatric disorders. Serotonin, dopamine, and norepinephrine are the particular chemicals that can be positively affected by the use of medication. In the field of psychopharmacology, where the most advances have been made in the last ten to fifteen years, the task, when there is an imbalance, is to restore equilibrium in the brain. This can only be done with the use of medication. This is an arduous job that requires experience and expertise since there is such variation from person to person in finding the right treatment to restore balance. For some, the ability to keep a reliable set point in their brain chemistry is seriously flawed, and treatment by medication is required in order to achieve balance.

Currently, diagnosis and treatment of brain disorders is an inexact science. For now, we must rely on behavioral observation and history to make an accurate diagnosis. For reasons that are not fully understood, this approach to diagnosis has had a high success rate for aiding in selecting a form of treatment that works. As more is learned about the brain, and more exact knowledge is obtained, we can be even more hopeful about reaching success in understanding and treating the conditions that prevent some children from achieving their potential.

There are very important reasons why more success in this field is a critical goal. People with brain disorders can have serious difficulty interacting with the rest of the world. Their behaviors are often unpleasant even to people who love them, making being with them a challenging and demanding experience. There may be many negative interactions and few positive ones. For the young person, there is a struggle to develop and maintain a degree of positive self-esteem and there is a higher incidence of school dropout behavior creating fewer positive prospects for successful earnings and employment.

Further, the normal developmental milestones are difficult to achieve or maintain. Some adolescents can't pay attention, don't have reliable friendships, and do not have satisfying relationships with their parents due to their inability to cooperate or interact pleasantly. With a brain disorder, it is hard for a child to develop positive relationships with teachers since the teacher finds it is hard to deal with the difficult and demanding behavior that accompanies the problem. In general, the adolescent's behavior critically affects the way she is regarded and treated in the outside world.

Some of the brain conditions currently being approached through diagnosis and treatment, as described by Koplewicz and others, include ADD, separation anxiety disorder, social phobia, generalized anxiety disorder and even more severe disorders. A child with a brain disorder has no time to lose. The longer she goes without treatment the longer she is exposed to the negative responses from the outside world that she can do nothing on her own to change. Parents, too, become increasingly demoralized and hopeless the longer there is no positive intervention that can observably help. Parents are in jeopardy of becoming seriously stressed and worn out and having their regard for their child critically eroded as each day goes by. They find their personal development blocked, marriages wrecked, and the struggle to get through each day overwhelming. On top of it all, they blame themselves for the problem.

Parents do have the responsibility for recognizing that there is a problem, and seeking out the right treatment. While they did not cause their child's difficulties, they must be single-minded in their dedication to doing everything possible to help their child become stabilized. If there are family issues complicating the problems or insufficient understanding of the developmental issues of adolescence creating awkward or ineffective parenting, family therapy may be indicated along with the other treatments described.

The first and most important task is to get a thorough psychiatric evaluation resulting in a working diagnosis. To achieve this task, parents need to seek out the best child psychiatrist available to them, one also experienced in adoption issues. This specialist must be skilled in coordinating the efforts of all the professionals that may be needed to work together to create a picture of the child that will result in a reliable diagnosis. Optimally, this professional should be highly experienced, empathetic and practiced at working in depth. Patience and creativity are qualities that aid the diagnostic process as well.

Pediatricians, social workers, psychologists, guidance counselors, educational consultants, other parents, as well as the local chapter of the American Psychiatric Association are usually good sources for finding a board certified child psychiatrist with a known ability for success in child diagnosis and treatment. Once an appointment has been made, the doctor will request any reports or evaluations that have already been done and suggest other evaluations if necessary, such as in the areas of neurology, psychology, speech, and language or hearing.

The parents will describe their concerns about the child's behavior and the doctor will take a thorough history. In some geographical areas, there may be non-medical therapists who are equally equipped to carry out a rigorous diagnostic evaluation. The final evaluation and resulting diagnosis will suggest a course of treatment, which may include medication, to be prescribed by a qualified psychiatrist. At this time, she will discuss with the parents the details and likelihood of success with various medications as she finds exactly the right balance for the adolescent.

The doctor or non-medical evaluator might suggest treatment for the child with a psychotherapist who specializes in childhood and adolescent therapy and who has knowledge of adoption and attachment issues. If there are learning issues, she might also suggest some form of tutoring or remediation or other intervention that will help the child gain ground and function closer to his peers socially, psychologically and academically.

In order for treatment to work, there must be a strong collaborative effort between parents and the treatment team. Parents need to learn about the disorder, understand it may have genetic underpinnings, be prepared to work hard to achieve success, and reach out for as much help as needed. Such resources as parent counseling, support groups, and individual and group therapy can be helpful in overcoming the malignant effects of years of unsuccessful struggle. Support groups, in particular, provide the opportunity to share experiences and strategies with parents who have gone through similar situations.

How does all of this help us to understand what has been operating with Bethany and add to an understanding of how Sara and John might have found help more quickly? How could they have relieved the almost unbearable stress they were under before the crisis Sara experienced that required the assistance of a medical team in her home?

The effort and attention that was given to Bethany and her issues was considerable from an early age. Sara describes in detail what she observed and did not know how to understand regarding the positives and negatives of Bethany's development. Many times Sara and John reached out for help and were told they were making too much of situations and that they should not worry so much. Even when Bethany was engaged in self-destructive behaviors as a teenager, teachers and other parents believed Bethany's stories that there was abuse and neglect at home, and gave Sara feedback indicating that she and John were at fault and should do things differently in order to be better parents. Bethany's ingratiating and manipulative behaviors that were key to her sense of survival allowed these misperceptions to persist and hindered movement towards a successful approach to treatment.

The psychoeducational evaluation conducted by the school psychologist when Bethany was almost sixteen continued this pattern. In this testing, Bethany is described as a "lonely, fearful, anxious and depressed young lady with a poor self-image." The emotional themes uncovered included describing Bethany as a "little girl whose dependency needs had been thwarted and who felt rejected, especially by the parents." It is more likely that Bethany's responses could be better understood as a reaction to feelings of early abandonment.

The summary provided little to no understanding of the actual interaction within the family and a lack of awareness of the dynamics of the attachment issues that operate in a life experience shaped by adoption. In fact, adoption is not mentioned at all as a dynamic in the evaluation, and the examiner did not appear to hear any of Bethany's responses in the light of adoption issues, even though projective testing brought out strong expressions of depression and emotional pain.

There were also rather striking academic issues commented on, such as below average reading comprehension, spelling ability, and large spreads between verbal and performance scores. The examiner commented on Bethany's high intelligence, but did not question her below average abilities in certain areas explaining this as being due to emotional reactions to her environment.

His interpretation was not unexpected. It was not unlike the two other therapists with whom the family had previously worked. The first therapist was seen in first grade when Bethany was stealing. The second was consulted when Bethany was in middle school and was with a group caught drinking on school grounds. In both instances, the therapists minimized the negative behavior, used traditional "talking therapy," and had no understanding or training in the issues of adoption and attachment theory. The day treatment program, which was at a prestigious adolescent treatment facility, followed the same pattern. None of the professionals involved appeared to understand the significance of the first year of life experiences and how Bethany had been impacted from her earliest days. Sara herself often questioned her own observations and tried to convince herself that the patterns she had seen since Bethany was a baby were perhaps inconsequential and that it was she who was making too much of things.

Had they then had the critically important information about infant bonding and attachment that we now have, Sara and John's parenting work with Bethany might have been less traumatic. While they observed her striking reactions to leaving her foster mother and coming to their home, they had no way to understand the implications of those reactions. While Bethany's suffering at that time was severe, it was far better than the experience she would have endured if she had not had the consistent and reliable first mothering experience with the foster mother, or if she had several moves in the first few months of life.

Under these circumstances, bonding and attachment would not have taken place at all. As it was, it appears that bonding did take place with Bethany's foster mother, and she described Bethany as a bright and happy baby. What occurred next was a break in that bonding when Bethany was moved to her adoptive home at the critical age of seven months. Such interruptions in the first year of life bring serious complications, which require years of attention if any headway is to be made towards repair. One of the most reliable signs of a break in attachment is a baby who does not want to be touched and held, who cries and arches her back when parents try to hold or hug her. Sara describes this reaction when Bethany came home.

But as Bethany grew, she showed signs of positive development. In the early years, she did well in school, was bright, independent and socially adept, even though she had certain undeniable behavioral difficulties. It was as Bethany reached puberty that her troublesome behaviors started to escalate.

No one will probably ever be able to answer with certainty the reasons why this was so, but it is likely that the disequilibria which naturally occurs in adolescence highlighted the attachment issues she had carried with her since infancy. Probably the pressure created for her was profound and made it impossible for her to hide any longer the struggle she had with her own pain—with the anxiety and depression she carried within her related to early loss.

All of this turmoil was complicated further by the stage of life at which the loss took place, which was preverbal. This made it impossible for Bethany to put the traumatic experiences into words so they could be expressed, identified, reexperienced, and understood.

In the book *High Risk* (1987), Dr. Ken Magid and Carole McKelvey tell us that unattached children cannot tolerate the limits placed on them by others. They are constantly testing and baiting to see what kind of reaction they will get. They may also have difficulty conforming to social norms, controlling impulses, tolerating frustration, identifying with others, profiting from corrective experiences or forming meaningful relationships.

After Sara and John took Bethany to a psychiatrist for evaluation in adolescence, they did receive a diagnosis of Oppositional Defiant Disorder and a prescription for medication. This came after a brief interview from a doctor who was neither thorough nor experienced in attachment issues, and Bethany did not benefit from this contact. She was later able to fool another professional she saw into believing she was just fine and her parents were the problem. This ability to be bright, charming, believable and independent is common ground for children and adolescents with attachment problems who know how to hide their issues well, and fool the outside world.

Manipulative behavior fits with their level of conscience development, which is weak at best, and understandably so, since conscience development is necessarily built on a solid base of trust and security, established in the first year of life. The negative compensation for the child in lacking this very important aspect of development involves being able to dodge any real connection to another person that would be based on honesty and reliability. That level of connection would allow the other person to become close and intimate and eventually see the emptiness and pain that is really there, instead of the grounding and growth towards maturity that one would hope for. Being seen this clearly is overwhelmingly frightening for the child or adolescent who is trying to hide. In Bethany's life, her precociousness and independent behavior early on clearly signaled *"Don't Touch!"*

If John and Sara had been more knowledgeable after it was clear that nothing had been gained from this latest medical intervention, a second opinion with a specialist in attachment problems might have been well placed. However, by this time, Bethany was almost sixteen years old and highly dedicated to resisting any positive response to the many interventions her parents had arranged in order to help her.

As her frantic behavior escalated, characterized by an inability to follow any rules, Sara and John had to face the inevitable and painful message—Bethany would have to leave home and experience another major separation in order to get the help she needed. For Sara and John, this move represented an effort to refocus Bethany's life away from the many destructive forces she faced every day. Still, even after this realization, it took considerable struggle to find an appropriate treatment setting and arrange for the necessary funding.

What Sara did learn is that there are treatment settings developed specifically for working with young people with attachment and related disorders. Most of these treatments usually require living away from home and being removed from the severe over stimulation of the adolescent peer group, and the opportunity to have too much space and too many choices. At last, the residential school would provide a place where Bethany would begin to slow down and enter into a treatment program aimed at repair. This two year period in a controlled setting was specifically designed to help Bethany become responsible for her behavior and her choices, to begin to use her resources to help her achieve success and, ultimately, to become a productive human being who could feel positively about herself and her achievements.

This choice was the very best choice available to the family for giving Bethany a chance to get her impulses under control so that she could lead an organized life, free from abusive and destructive behaviors and the influences of drugs and alcohol. Once that was accomplished, she would be able to get on an organized and controlled path, stop running and hiding, and begin to behave along more conventional lines. This meant that she would now be going to school regularly, earning good grades, and participating in healthy aspects of community life. After accomplishing all of that, she would be able to enter into a treatment plan that could help her build the bonds of attachment that she would need in order to have a satisfying adult life and commit herself to her own welfare and the rebuilding of her self-esteem.

8

TACKLING THE PROBLEM: WHAT WORKS

"Get rid of her posters and her music, the clothing and trash. When Bethany comes home you don't want her to see any of the reminders of her former negative life."

Our drive to the school was a quiet one. Bethany had been told to leave her electronic paraphernalia behind, so the muffled sounds of thumping headphones that we were used to hearing from the back of the car were absent. Up front, we kept the radio silent too, preferring to mull over our own private thoughts.

In my fortress of silence, I thought about all of the recent events and how we had gotten to this point. My mind tortured itself with, "If I hadn't done this" or "If she only did that." I needed to convince myself repeatedly that we were saving her life. It became my mantra, "You're saving her life!" "You're saving her life!" giving me the confidence I needed so badly.

As I fortified myself, I thought of the many people who routinely send their children to boarding school, but I knew this was different. Bethany would be reading this as punishment for her destructive behavior and another abandonment that she would have to endure. And for my part, I knew I would be missing out on her teenage years, a time normally fraught with drama and tension, but also an optimum age to be imparting parental lessons and sharing wonderful and memorable mother and daughter memories. We would never get those years together and we would never be able to make up for their loss. On the other hand, what we were living through now was nothing that any one of us would care to memorialize. Hopefully, in the future, when we looked back on this time, we would be able to focus on the success of the plan, and she would understand why we made the sacrifice.

Bethany slept noisily in the back, breathing loudly, totally exhausted by what we hoped was her final fling. She hadn't slept at all the night before, and her life had been so wild leading up to this event, that her body and her soul were worn out. She had told us repeatedly. "I don't know why I do these things. I don't want to, but I can't help myself." Now I kept looking behind me to try to read her mind, hoping I would get a glimmer of understanding from her. What I saw instead was a shrouded figure. She wore a dark blue hooded sweatshirt pulled up over her head hiding most of her face from my gaze. Her skin was chalky white. Curled up in a fetal position, hugging her pillow she seemed so vulnerable, and I once again wondered if there wasn't another way that we could stop her from destroying herself. Was this the thing to do? Would this stop her and allow her to look at herself and her future and the world? My brain told me that I did not have the luxury of choice. It was this or ... I couldn't let my mind complete the thought.

As we drove up to the school, a statue of the Virgin Mary welcomed us. Inside, the building was decorated with banners and signs proclaiming the virtues of love, honesty, purity and unselfishness. I did not register the words, only the image. Student artwork, most of it of a religious nature, was occasionally displayed as a reminder to students of their place in the world order, and trophy cases lined the walls with awards for a variety of sports and musical achievements. The floors and walls were spotless; the light was bright so that everything was well illuminated.

Going into a public school one always is impressed by the noise and hubbub. Students sporting a variety of dress styles will be screaming, shoving, joking and running between classes. Here the kids were enthusiastic, smiling and joking, but the tones were more hushed and the currently popular fashion trends were not apparent. Instead they wore conservative clothing, well fitting and modestly presented—no baggy jeans, no sloppy t-shirts, and no inappropriate tops. I was impressed with the intelligent conversation and happy faces of the kids.

I wanted so badly to find help here, but I was uncomfortable too. First, I knew that all of the children here had stories similar to Bethany's, no matter how intelligent they sounded. Second, the sloganeering made me ill at ease. I thought of George Orwell and his presentation of the slogans touting totalitarian principles and the use the Chinese made of their propagandizing slogans during the Cultural Revolution. And the religious overtones made me uncomfortable too. I wanted my children to act from their own well-developed consciences and intellects, not because they were afraid of punishment.

But I could not risk Bethany's life with my sophomoric arguments. We were bringing our child here to save her life, and I would have to live with my discomfort. And, in fact, I could not deny that the slogans here made sense. They had four principles: Honesty, Purity, Unselfishness, and Absolute Love. We had always tried to emphasize these same ideals of honesty, unselfishness, and love to our children. We added respect for others so our basic thinking was not very far apart, but clearly our free thinker approach to life was not working. Perhaps these children needed to have these values put front and center in their lives. Maybe this method of child rearing was exactly what she needed, and what we had missed! So I swallowed my doubts as I was to do many times during those two years, and we headed toward the office with Bethany looking at none of the surroundings and totally unaware of my distress.

I don't know what she was aware of. Her shoulders were hunched up defensively and she remained silent when we walked through the office towards the Admissions desk. In this stance, she could not have seen anything, not even the director who introduced himself to her. He was a very imposing man, at least six and a half feet tall, with a mustache and a fairly large girth. I'm pretty sure she was intimidated when she finally lifted her head at the sound of his resonant voice and probably intentionally so. It was important that she quickly learn her place.

Shortly, two students arrived who would be checking her belongings for contraband and confiscating what the school deemed inappropriate. One of the girls was my former student who had been specifically chosen by the staff to orient Bethany. It made me feel somewhat more comfortable, but again, I could not read my daughter.

While they were going through this procedure, the Admissions Director was explaining some of the rules to us and reminding us that we would not be able to speak to her for at least six weeks. We could get updates from him if we wanted to call, but there could be no contact between Bethany and us. In the meantime, he urged us to spend the time repairing our own relationship and ridding the house of Bethany's former life. "Get rid of her posters and her music, the clothing and trash. When Bethany comes home you don't want her to see any of the reminders of her former negative life."

Whereas Bethany came to the school with resignation, other students came to the school in differing moods. Some were raging in anger; others threatened to kill themselves. None of them came looking forward to the experience and to the rigorous regimen that they were going to begin. Bethany knew little about the program, being unwilling to hear when we tried to prepare her and never having been the most attentive listener anyway. I assume she didn't listen when the director spoke to her in those first moments either. "More Blah! Blah! Blah!" from the adult world, she would be thinking. Perhaps our being there was also a distraction from her ability to focus on what she needed to know, so they urged us to leave quickly, and she could begin. Bethany returned to the office and was told we were leaving. She wouldn't kiss me good-bye or even look at us. My heart was broken, and I wanted to explain it all to her, but of course, I couldn't, and we left not knowing what she was feeling.

The drive home was mostly silent. Sometimes I would ask John what he thought she was thinking or if this was really a good place for her, but he had no good answers. When we returned home I went straight to her room. It was unbearable, so I shut the door and crawled into bed. Meanwhile, John went to work. He filled eight trash bags with cigarette butts, love letters, threatening notes, phone lists, Tampax, pizza boxes, paper plates, size 42 inch jeans, more unsent notes, torn t-shirts, stolen underwear with inventory tags still intact, broken cassette tapes, the dregs of her past life.

The first week was very difficult. My instinct was to call everyday. When I woke up I thought of her and wanted to call to see how she was doing and how she was sleeping. Bethany had been plagued with nightmares since she was a little girl, and I worried about her waking up in strange surroundings unable to get her bearings when she woke up. Later, I wanted to call her when I returned home from work to see how her day had gone. I had a million questions: Was she making friends? Was she afraid? Was she eating? Was she able to do the schoolwork? What were they reading? What were the other kids like and the teachers?

Matt was away at school, and I hesitated to call him because I knew he was unhappy with our decision. I didn't want to agitate him and distract him from his schoolwork. As far as he was concerned, she wasn't doing anything outrageous, "In fact" he said, "most teenagers do those kinds of things today." But we had protected him from the whole truth, and he didn't understand the extent of her degradation.

I think I controlled myself and called only three times the first week always to ask, "How is she?"

"She's doing fine!" There were never any complaints about her behavior or her adjustment. I was somewhat surprised. In her previous schools, it had not taken long for her to rebel against the demands of the program, and the calls would come about her cursing out her teachers or refusing to do the work. But now there was nothing.

"Has she tried to run away?" I asked.

"No, nothing like that. She's doing everything she has to do. She seems to be adjusting just fine."

With each call I made I expected to hear the worst but it didn't happen. Bethany seemed to be fitting in. Later I would learn why. Bethany was learning to navigate in her new setting, and she was going to tread very carefully. What she saw was that kids who violated any of the rules were singled out, and the school used it as an opportunity for learning or what the Chinese would have called reeducation. Bethany hated playing that kind of role; she wanted invisibility.

The school ran a behavioral modification program. Negative behavior was punished, and positive behavior was rewarded. The ultimate goal was to have these wayward kids, oppositionally defiant with their disordered temperaments, develop healthy and solid consciences. To accomplish this, the school had to separate the kids from their past. Friends, music, clothing, behaviors were all "triggers" for their negative behaviors, and just one exposure could set off a chain of events that put these kids' lives in jeopardy. In order to separate them from the triggers, the school needed parental cooperation. That was why we were interviewed and not Bethany. The program couldn't work if we weren't in agreement with its approach and technique. So the students were physically cut off and the process began.

What is necessary to develop a functioning conscience? A strong authority figure—the school providing a set of principles to live by—four slogans, or a twelve-step program, or the Ten Commandments. These had to be made part of a person's persona. She had to understand the difference between right and wrong, good and bad, impulsive, and well thought out. Along with their principles, the school had a solid program. Between the work, school, and spiritual segments, the day was filled, allowing no idle time. Students lived in modular units with fourteen residing in each one. At 5:00 AM, they awoke and took a quick timed shower in the one bathroom that they left in spotless condition. Then they dressed and went to the chapel or to one of the earlier jobs. From there they went to classes, then sports and the arts which might be painting, music, drama or dance. At 5:00 PM, they went to dinner and then study hall and peer tutoring.

During meals they had "table talk." This could be intense. Questions could emerge from any facet of a youngster's life and if the kids didn't find the topics for discussion the supervisors would. It was very personal. At each meal a different person was called up. Nobody among the students was exempt, and nobody looked forward to being the topic of discussion. Questions were varied:

"Why did you leave the bathroom so messy?"

"Why did you fail your math test?"

"What did you do when you went home this weekend?"

"Why do you steal from your parents?"

"What are you thinking about when you are standing here being screamed at?"

One question lead to another while the inquisitors uncovered the truth and tried to have the young person accept responsibility for his actions.

One of the things Bethany had always complained of was that we were always screaming at her. In truth, we had stopped screaming long ago and now just stated matter-of-factly what angered us. She was hearing the screaming in her own head. These kids, many of them anyway, perceived any criticism as screaming. The kid who had been called up for such an inquisition would quickly try to deflect the attention from himself by confessing to some minor infraction. He would then spend time explaining how much he had learned and how he appreciated that everyone was being honest with him. With relief, the young man in the spotlight would assure everyone that all of this talk "really made him feel good." You could see in his face the hope that this was the end of it, but his interrogators were always as smart as he was, having been guilty of similar transgressions and having endured similar questioning not too many days before. They would badger the subject with follow up questions until lies and easy answers were revealed and repudiated, and the truth came out. And if it didn't, there were steps that followed. It was a hard and painful process and was meant to help the kids see how negative and self-centered their behavior was.

Rules were very clear at the school and consistently enforced. Everyone eats full portions. There are no special meals. You do all of your homework, take all of your tests, attend all of your classes; no excuses were accepted. Socially, the students were not allowed to form cliques or to engage in boy/girl relationships beyond classes and meals. If friendships got too tight, the school would separate the two friends to minimize the chance of an unholy alliance being formed.

If you broke the rules you lost your privileges—calls home, home visits, recreation time, school trips. Students who were less firm in their commitment to the program were assigned "shadows," other students who acted as their consciences and mentors. And they were all responsible for each other, being obligated to help their peers make the proper decisions, and if they couldn't do that, bringing their behaviors up for communal discussion. Everyone participated in a sport and other activity and was given all sorts of opportunities to excel. Bethany played volleyball and the drums in the school band. Student jobs were varied: cleaning, cooking, working in the laundry, gardening. Bethany's favorite was cooking breakfast because the atmosphere was somewhat more relaxed, but all of the jobs demanded proficiency.

The curriculum supported the focus on ethics. Course work was value centered so the reading and the writing usually had a moral component. Every adult on the campus was involved in each student's growth, and by the time students had completed the program they were to have developed a strong moral code, allegiance to a healthy peer group and pride in their achievements.

The school had taken over our role, acting in loco parentis, providing structure, discipline, goals and values. Unfettered by a sense of failure and impending doom, they were able to move ahead and provide Bethany and the others with a sense of morality and help her discover her unique potential. Her goals were slowly evolving into dreams for her life, and we, in turn, were cautiously renewing our dreams for her.

◆   ◆   ◆

Bethany is now fifteen, in the peak of mid-adolescent turmoil. She is lost and has not been able to find her way. Sara and John have accompanied her each step on this journey, trying to find the key to what will help her calm down and focus on a positive and healthy life. Nothing has worked in spite of countless attempts to provide direction and fresh starts. Bethany appears to be beaten by her own internal upheaval, and Sara and John have felt sad, angry, depressed, bewildered and in danger of losing hope. What has happened here, and what are the possible outcomes? How will all of this affect Bethany's future life? What will help stop the frantic downward spiral? Exhausted, they have made a decision for treatment that will include the long avoided separation from home in order to promote development.

Bethany has long displayed many of the symptoms of attachment disorder. There is also the possibility of non-diagnosed ADHD. The severity of the attachment condition is at the high end of the scale, which occurs along a continuum from mild to severe. Terry M. Levy and Michael Orlans in their book *Attachment Trauma and Healing* (1998, 76) have provided us with a definitive body of knowledge about attachment issues—causes, symptoms, and treatment. They have written specifically about the correlation of attachment with ADHD and bipolar disorder, and the high incidence of these conditions in children who are adopted. Levy and Orlans have paid special attention to the role of the adoptive parents and the critical need for these parents to be realistic and highly committed to the task of working towards helping their child achieve mental health. Parents certainly cannot "fix" their children, but can work to build a family environment that will be most likely to facilitate optimal growth.

In some states there are requirements for adoptive parents to take classes and spend a specific number of hours in training before they can adopt a child. This is a positive forward step in assisting these parents in their complicated parenting roles. The training focuses on understanding the importance of healthy emotional development during the first eighteen months of life. The course also describes the attachment cycle, including how to recognize childhood grief and identify the signs of attachment throughout the developmental stages.

Newborns of mothers who are depressed during pregnancy are more irritable, have less developed muscle tone, and are less consolable. Parenting workshops help prepare adoptive parents for understanding these possibilities and developing strategies for working with them.

What about Bethany? What has gone wrong? Where has development been arrested? What is the key to what will allow her to move forward? Not knowing anything about Bethany's genetic background complicated Sara and John's task in finding answers to these questions.

As we know, the move from her foster home to her adoptive home was hard and Bethany showed signs of difficulty in adjusting which was unavoidable under the circumstances, especially given her age of seven months at placement. As she continued to grow and develop, it was often hard to tell if there were long term difficulties from the move, but there were many warning signs—things that made Sara and John uneasy.

In the 1980s, there were significant discoveries about the human brain and the central nervous system. One area of interest has been the role of the brain's limbic system in modulating emotions and behavior. The limbic system, located deep in the human brain, is associated with survival instincts and basic primitive emotions such as rage, fear and aggression. Traumatizing experiences, such as early loss of the mother, appear to become encoded in this primitive, non-verbal part of the brain causing automatic brain responses to fear. It can also cause behaviors such as lying and unexplained aggression, difficulty modulating affect, withdrawal, avoidance of intimacy, and memory disorganization. The child's willingness to be dependent on the parents may be strongly resisted. When early trauma has occurred, brain activity is centered in this more primitive area, and evolution to the next stage of development in the prefrontal area of the brain is impeded (James 1994, 14–15).

The prefrontal lobes, located in the front of the brain are the most evolved part of the human brain. This area is associated with higher qualities such as idealism, joy, focus, creativity, and abstract thought. Also dependent on the prefrontal lobes are happiness and the ability to enjoy life.

Important questions arise about brain function regarding which methods can be used to develop the prefrontal lobes towards the goal of achieving a more calm, centered approach to life. Meditation is thought to be one method of centering and quieting the mind which also provides better integration, reduces levels of depression and anxiety, promotes better social skills, and enhances self-control and creativity.

The practice of meditation, as well as yoga and karate, and other techniques that control physical activity, provide high forms of structure for brain activity. During meditation brainwave patterns and brain chemistry change significantly and stress hormone levels drop.

Bethany did not learn to meditate during her time away from home at the residential school. What she did learn was how to live a highly structured life where expectations were clear and unbendable. She was surrounded by peers who had earlier experiences similar to hers and knew her language. They challenged her approach to life on a daily basis. She was also expected to challenge her peers and confront any unwillingness on their parts to choose a more disciplined form of behavior and thinking. Surrounded by a staff of adults who were dedicated to her growth and rigid in their expectations of her performance, she was guided towards a life of ethical behavior and dedication to truth and honesty.

Bethany was in this environment for two years while she completed her junior and senior years of high school. Was she happy? Did she adapt to this life, this way of thinking, this approach to developing into a caring, empathetic, ethical young woman? We know that she calmed down when she was removed from the cultural influences of a chaotic social life, which had encouraged her to be completely out of control. In her new school, she was forced to stop her wild flailing around and adapt to an environment that was structured and aimed at developing a sense of responsibility and self-monitoring.

At the school, there were systems, routines, and rituals. Jobs and involvement in sports and activities were demanded. Achievements were recognized, and there was reinforcement for jobs well done. Doing one's best was encouraged; mediocrity was not accepted. Positive actions and thoughts were supported. Negative thoughts and actions were unacceptable. There was a strong sense of community and mutual responsibility.

The school became the surrogate mother. Through the process of making rules, having a tight leash, setting up systems, the environment for developing an internalization process was organized. Bethany had the opportunity to quiet the part of herself that was overwhelmed by too much noise, too much over stimulation of every kind and be surrounded with expectations for doing her best and fulfilling her capabilities. She was given the opportunity to minimize the pressure she had felt all of her life which became uncontrollable during her teenage years and concentrate on the qualities that could make her calmer, happier, more in control of her thoughts and actions. The environment provided the opportunity to accept the possibility that she could trust those close to her and that she could believe that good things would come her way through her own hard work and reliability.

At the school, Bethany had the opportunity to develop a reliable inner mother as described in Chapter 4. When this process takes place we can remember the good mother and carry her with us when we are away from her. We are developing the ability for self-soothing and comfort, the ability for ethical and compassionate behavior, a reliable conscience. When this process goes wrong we will have difficulty loving others, taming our aggressions, developing empathy. When it goes right, we will have a sense of hopefulness that the world is a good place and we are safe in it, and we become more able to make good choices for ourselves.

Children who have the early trauma of troubled pregnancy and separation from their mothers have undeniable symptoms of posttraumatic stress disorder including grief issues, that are often manifested in Reactive Attachment Disorder. Unable to overcome these stresses on their own, they cannot progress smoothly through the stages of development. This task will be impossible to achieve without a blueprint for help through the trouble spots and an intimate understanding of the problem by parents and involved adults.

If indeed a child is to move through the stages of development with some success, she first must learn to become attached to and bonded with a trustworthy mother figure. She will learn from that mother how to trust that her needs will be taken care of. She will learn to know when to hold on and when to let go. She will learn with confidence when to say "yes" and when to say "no." She will learn to control her urges and to take pleasure in performing well. She will eventually learn how to take her good mother with her, inside of her, to monitor and control and manage her environment. She will learn how to care for people's feelings and how to take care of others. She will learn how to do a job well, how to have a sense of competence. She will naturally evolve, in Erikson's term, a sense of industry. This sense of industry, he asserts, is what develops a lasting basis for cooperative participation in productive adult life.

Through the development of these abilities, conscience is born, ethics are developed and a sense of personal identity, an "I am" is achieved. When these goals are not reached or are interrupted, there is a sense of identity confusion, and an inability to feel any confidence about who one is and how one fits into the world. One of the most important aspects of learning how to develop identity Erikson believes, is settling on an occupation with the accompanying feeling,

"This is what I do well, and this is what I have to offer the world." The inability to settle on an occupational identity is perhaps the most difficult obstacle to maturity for many young people.

One of the final achievements in development is the ability for true intimacy with another, which can only come when one is sure of a stable personal identity. This attainment of intimacy is a feeling of being open to and bonded to another while maintaining a sense of separate self.

It is easy to see how Bethany's development was interrupted in critical ways in her first year and how these interruptions affected her ability to move through the stages of development in spite of her parents' best efforts. In order to provide the climate that Bethany needed to overcome the effects of early trauma she would have to be isolated from the confusion of a daily experience filled with overwhelming and inappropriate stimulation when she reached adolescence. In order to provide this setting, John and Sara had to make the decision to have Bethany live away from home in a place that had the ability to exert maximum control over the environment. The school was able to surround Bethany with a unified message and a way of reinforcing the message, over and over, until it could be heard over the clamor of her internal din. There are various ways to achieve this goal, but all require long term opportunity for exposure to a lifestyle that promotes the ability to internalize a stable self. Bethany was able to make use of this form of treatment and make gains in her development in the time frame available to her. It was a good beginning.

9

EPILOGUE

*"As her confidence is growing, she is opening herself up to the world
of positive experiences."*

I personally hate books that don't have endings, even though my life has taught
me that there are none. Life is always moving, ebbing and flowing, and from my
vantage point, I know that a second can make the difference in the way things
turn out. What looks hopeless and beyond repair right this minute, can be aston-
ishingly altered in the intake of a breath. So it has been with Bethany's life. I will
use the next few pages to describe her, now twenty-five years old, and our family
today.

As Bethany entered her new school, we were hopeful that she was going to this
wonderful safe place where they would restore all the goodness that she had been
born with. She would become self-confident, honorable, energetic, creative, and a
positive force for herself and the world. And we would all live happily-ever-after.
That is what we all wanted to believe, and oh, that it was only so.

But, of course, this is real life, and things don't go as evenly as that. After two
years at the school, she graduated with a sense of how it could feel to live with
ethics and purpose. The school taught her moral principles to help her with difficult choices and modeled the questions she should be asking herself so that she
could modify her behavior. They taught her how to study and achieve excellence
in every aspect of her life; they set the groundwork so that she could focus on
meaningful goals. At her graduation, Bethany was left with a permanent picture
of what she should be aiming for. She was fortified with a solid academic background, good study skills and a sense of purpose. She had good grades, decent
test scores, exemplary extra-curricular activities, community service and many
varied experiences. But most of all, she learned that she had the capacity to work
hard to successfully accomplish what had seemed to be an impossible challenge.
That summer Bethany came home to what we hoped would be a time of reflection and preparation for college. She took a summer job at a camp, stayed sober

and returned home every night as we had insisted. But it still wasn't right. Many of her former friends resurfaced and with them the memories of all that had happened in the past.

We tried to bolster her confidence by reminding her of all of her successes, and we reinforced the information that there would be plenty of systems in place to support her if she ran into trouble, but we had our doubts about her commitment to using them. Not wanting to plant any more seeds for failure, we kept many of our concerns silent, believing that our confidence in her would be more helpful than our doubts, but our misgivings did not go away.

The summer passed and we watched her summer reading assignment get buried under more and more layers of clothing. When she ignored our urgings to contact her soon to be college roommate a red flag went up, so even the knowledge that she had the skills and ability necessary for success did not mollify our concerns.

The metaphor of the elephant in the room works here; everyone knows it is there but no one will talk about it. There were still untapped areas which she had never explored and which were lurking in the background. Though we had pressed the school to explore her "issues," the school had declined to do this, focusing on her current behaviors. They did this with all of their students. Her insecurities relating to adoption and rejection and her impulsive and negative behavior were only examined from a moral point of view. The message was that "you made these choices and you need to make better ones." We did not disagree with that thinking and knew that if she didn't learn how to moderate her conduct, anything else would be meaningless.

We were rightly concerned that at no time were her psychic wounds probed. At the school, there had been minimal individual counseling and little family therapy. So when she graduated, she was still an unfinished work. She had not yet begun the task of psychological and emotional development expected at this stage. (See Developmental Benchmarks) It would take the years after that graduation to complete that work so that she would examine the motivation behind her behaviors.

We had the sense that there was pent up energy inside her that was screaming to get out. We were fearful she would not make it through the summer, but happily, she did.

After her summer vacation, she nervously left home headed to a good college where many options would be open to her but silently fearful that she could not succeed. Many times before she had set out with good intentions only to give up at the first obstacle she encountered. She did not trust herself, and she was terrified that she would fail again.

Why wouldn't someone who knew she was vulnerable reach out for help that had been freely offered? When she was preparing to leave high school, her advisor had urged her to continue to attend AA meetings at college, but she refused. She also ignored the academic support that was available there. Old behaviors resurfaced immediately. She cut classes doing who knows what, and she turned to her old boyfriend who provided a strong link to home. Every weekend she returned to be with him or he visited her on campus. She never truly asserted her independence nor did she explore the school's diverse offerings, even though she expressed interest. By the time her soccer coach tried to mentor and redirect her, the consequences of her behavior were irreparable. She was already too deep into the failure cycle to stop its momentum, and by the New Year, she was back home with us.

But we were not the same people any more. We had learned a lot from our experience and were realistic about how much control we had. Now the parents of an adult daughter, we knew she was the one who would have to live with the responsibilities of her age. We spelled out our expectations and stood behind them. She would have to work, take courses, and keep communicating with us. That meant if she was not coming home we expected to be notified ahead of time so that there were no sleepless nights waiting for unimaginable phone calls. In return, she could live in our house.

The plan worked for only a few months. Bethany held a job and showed that she could be responsible, but the other areas appeared to be beyond her abilities. Consequently, we gave her three months to find another place to live and so ended that phase of her life.

What she found was her boyfriend's family, who graciously took her in, charmed by her intelligence, good manners, and apparent ability to negotiate a difficult world. They were in awe of her energy and the way she seemed to be able to take control, and they were good, loving people. She moved in to their home and stayed until the two could afford a place on their own.

And then began the independent adult phase of her life. No, not yet. Over a year passed and she held a job and was competent in fulfilling its responsibilities. For a while she enjoyed fixing up the apartment and playing house but then, at some point, she became bored with both the job and the boyfriend. It was not long before she got caught up in another downward spiral that involved the same old pattern compounded with unpaid speeding tickets, overdue bills, late night disappearances, erratic behavior at work. Eventually we got another phone call, "I need help." It was hard for her to make that phone call, I am sure of that. She had been convinced of her adulthood, and now she had messed up again. Everything that had started out so well had slowly disintegrated. When she felt her relationship with her boyfriend ending painfully, it became too much for her to handle.

Our response was immediate. "You can come home to live. You can use the time to get your life back in order." For several weeks she mulled the offer over while more bills accumulated and, by now, she had lost her job. She had few options.

I saw so clearly then that very young child who while exploring the world keeps checking in to see that her mother is still there. This behavior was several years late in coming, but nevertheless, I recognized the pattern.

Bethany moved back and we gave her a few simple rules about living in someone else's house that she accepted. The Bethany who returned was completely different from the one we had last lived with. This one was ready for some mothering. The years out on her own had given her an appreciation for us, our life's choices, and our relationships. The new Bethany now wanted to be part of the family. She joined us at mealtime, sometimes even cooking and trying new recipes. She cheerily helped with chores, even taking on a few of her own. She was engaging and fun to be with. We spent time together discussing our lives, talking about friends, planning parties, even taking on "serious" subjects like books and world affairs. At various times, we talked about adoption, searching, the possibility that Bethany had ADD, and other personal subjects that we rarely touched on before. What had begun as another disaster was turning into a new opportunity to heal the bonds that had been broken. Her failure was leading to the restoration of our relationships and the eventual healing of our family.

Bethany is now an adult and on her own journey. It may never be a straight and determined course, but she is moving in a forward and positive direction. She has a wonderful job that she loves and that loves her. She feels creative and productive and smart, and she works with people who enjoy what they do and do it well. She recognizes and appreciates the value in this. For her part, her boss values her work and is quick to praise her for all the complex tasks she takes on and completes. This alone has raised her self-confidence. And the other benefits are uncountable. She's cheerful and proud and beginning to take her place in the world. She is meeting people who have achieved educationally and vocationally, and are also fun to be with. They include her in many social get togethers and she is happy to be there.

Bethany is also back in school, slowly working toward her educational goals. She is aware of her shortcomings, is a much stronger person than she was before, and has learned a lot about herself. There are still some bumps in her way. Sticking with a task or goals remains problematic but she is working on that. She still doesn't like quiet activity. She prefers action and a faster life style; although, having realized the consequences of impulsive behavior she has toned down these urges considerably. She is more respectful of our needs, keeps in touch, contributes to family life, and celebrates family events. She works hard to be honest and is appreciative of ethical standards in other people.

Our significant parenting role continues. There are still goals left for Bethany to accomplish before she successfully lives on her own. The struggle to find her own identity and further integrate all of her different parts continues. She refuses to reenter therapy to help her with this task, but on her own she has worked hard to accomplish this goal. We have learned to cherish the steps she takes toward success. We see this as a unique opportunity to complete our job. In this time, we can celebrate her triumphs with her, but we can't ever stop talking about the difficult decisions that she is faced with making everyday revolving around relationships, adult responsibilities, and planning for the future.

In the past, we have seen her growth emerge after a devastating defeat, and now we see her triumphs coming more frequently and from her own ability to make good choices. We know that she values our love and trusts that we will be there for her, providing stability when she feels insecure. As time transpires, we find ourselves more likely to trust her, and we become more hopeful that she will achieve all of the independence that she needs to make her way in this world and to contribute as an adult to society and her own happiness.

◆   ◆   ◆

The years for Bethany between high school graduation and the age of twenty-five have been years of slow growth, zigzagging developmental ups and downs, and painstaking movement towards age and stage appropriate stability.

Although they have often felt like giving up, Sara and John have come to understand and even embrace the idea that Bethany has needed these years with them to allow for the parenting that has occurred and could not have been experienced earlier when the necessary underpinnings were not yet in place. Because they found a balance between being available to provide love and a listening ear with the boundaries that provided structure for Bethany's conscience development, she has been able to rely more and more on her own judgment and make better decisions for herself, as Sara has described.

Bethany now wants to do the right thing even though she cannot always manage to do so. She is interested in her own moral and ethical standards and those of others.

One of the important aspects of Bethany's life with her parents at this stage has been her experience of moving in and out of the family home several times. She found the opportunity freely offered by her parents, but not without the expectation of responsible behavior on her part. When she could not adhere to the expectations set out for her, she was asked to move out. She found herself not being able to exist for long in the more intimate family setting before she would have to distance herself by demonstrating that she could not be a part of the routine and ritual experienced by the other members of the family. Yet, each time Bethany has moved back into the house, she has been more successful at taking part in family life.

In the last year or two, Bethany has succeeded in getting and keeping a responsible, interesting, job in a professional office where she has demonstrated a number of the skills she possesses and where she is highly valued by her employer and co-workers. She is admired and praised for her work and included in social get togethers. Through this experience she has a growing sense of her own worth and motivation to continue to improve and develop further.

For the first time, Bethany is in a college course which she is completing. She has more patience now for sticking with something even when it is less than exciting, and seeing it through to the end. She seems aware of the value of education for her, and of her ability to succeed in this area.

Bethany has remained committed to an ongoing relationship with her boyfriend who has provided her with companionship, approval, stability and a sense of safety. That he is attached to a large and extended, warm family that makes no demands on her is also appealing to her. While she is clearly the leader in that relationship, carrying out the style she has experienced with males since her teens, she does seem to be more grounded than if she was not connected to a partner. Developmentally, it is notable that Bethany has not chosen to push for marriage or parenthood as yet, in spite of the intense internal pressure to do so that is often experienced by adopted adults.

Although Bethany has several long-term friendships with girlfriends, they seem to lack the intimacy that many women find in these relationships. This absence is not well described, but can be seen in light of her need to spend all of her free time with a significant male partner who can take the place of the early mothering figures from whom she had to prematurely separate. Perhaps never having been given the opportunity to mourn these losses she has not been able to trust that these female relationships would be safe and reliable. She has, however, been able to be closer and more intimate with Sara and has clearly shown her need for and her enjoyment of this aspect of their relationship.

Bethany's relationship with John is friendly and affectionate, and includes talking and a mutual interest in sports and music. She comes to him for advice about how to handle various situations and clearly loves and respects him. She also seems to be a little wary of him since he speaks very directly to her about her choices and behaviors and is not inclined to give her much room for repetitious mistakes in her actions.

In comparison to her adolescent days when Bethany was combative and refused to deal at all with John, and tried to pit her parents against each other, Bethany now feels her parents have a perfect relationship, characterized by harmony and cooperation. She does not have a memory of the days of conflict and strain among other members of the family, in part because she absented herself so frequently from her home. Now this new position is helping her to continue her development as she shows an awareness of the realities of a resilient marriage relationship that can withstand conflict.

Although Bethany does not spend a large amount of time with her brother, Matt, because their interests are so varied and their free time often does not coincide, they still enjoy the time they do spend together. She appears to feel about him much as she did when she met him in the first year of life. She trusts him, appreciates him, admires him and always wants to know where he is and what he is doing. She thinks of him in superlatives—hilarious, brilliant and handsome.

Matt appears to love and care for his sister as well, but is not as trusting of her as she is of him due to her past pattern of unreliability. The differences in their development seem to be in the variability in impulsive thought and behavior and the struggle Bethany has had to develop a reliable conscience.

Since her years in therapy as an adolescent, Bethany has again tried to enter into a therapeutic relationship, but could not sustain it past a few months, even though this beginning was positive, and she liked and respected her therapist. She may not yet be ready to take a deeper look at her inner world with the awareness and hurts that will come as she gets in touch with early life experiences. As she grows older, she may enter into a stage which demands greater self-knowledge in order to continue to grow. Or she may find herself strong enough to be confident that she can enter into a therapeutic relationship and gain inner calm and stability from the experience. In the meantime, she is on a path of self-discovery through her experience of success in work, school, and family life. As her confidence is growing, she is opening herself up to the world of positive experiences.

For those whose life experiences have not been as extreme as Bethany's, the dynamic of loss and grieving are nevertheless ongoing issues of bonding and attachment which will play a significant role in their continuing development in adult life and adult relationships. Understanding and support from parents and family can make a significant difference in achieving a stable adult identity.

One of the things we have learned from Bethany and other adopted young adults, is that development and growth towards maturity takes longer than the average timetable and is much more precarious along the way. The detours and delays are abundant and for many the road towards a stable identity is not as successful as it has been for Bethany. While she will always be vulnerable around the experiences of loss and while she may question her ability to have reliable ongoing relationships, she has demonstrated a wish to be a valued, responsible person. She has also demonstrated an ability to work towards that goal.

Sara and John have been committed to being hopeful, positive, available, and accepting of Bethany's struggles. They have developed their own lives and have given their daughter the support and role models she needs in order to develop hers. The next few years hold the possibility for deepening and strengthening her sense of grounding so she can experience herself as a fully developed adult.

DEVELOPMENTAL BENCHMARKS

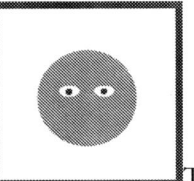FETUS at five months—12 billion nerve cells—full quota for human nervous system. As fetus grows, nerve cells organizing in various patterns determine behavior.

FIRST YEAR OF LIFE-NEONATAL (birth to four weeks)— Primary mental growth accomplished, expressions of individuality apparent, well advanced adjustment to postnatal environment, responds to mother's face and voice.

TWELVE WEEKS—Gains control over eye muscles.

SIXTEEN to TWENTY-EIGHT WEEKS—Controls muscles which support head, moves arms, reaches, sits, recognizes mother, vivid smile, beginning to focus attention, handles small toy for long period and preoccupied with solitary activity, attachment to single caretaker.

TWENTY-EIGHT to FORTY WEEKS—Command of trunk and hands, sits, grasps, transfers and manipulates objects, ability to perceive strangeness, parent deemed irreplaceable.

FORTY to FIFTY-TWO WEEKS—Controls legs and feet, forefinger and thumb, pokes and plucks, stands upright, likes people around, ability to perceive strangers, can play by self for an hour.

TWELVE MONTHS—More conscious of surroundings, displays variety of emotions, primitive sense of humor, responds to music, likes to be center of attention and draw laughs, adaptive to other's emotions, brain becomes regulated for calming down with organizing and soothing help.

EIGHTEEN MONTHS to TWO YEARS—Uses words and phrases, bowel and bladder control developing, budding sense of personal identity and awareness of personal possessions, claims *Mine*, understands you and me, walks and runs, leading to more mature psychological state of separateness from mother which includes frequent checking in for comfort and support and then running off for exploration of world.

THIRD YEAR—Uses words to express thought, speaks in sentences, understands surroundings and often cooperates with adult expectations.

FOURTH YEAR—Asks questions, displays ability to build concepts and understands how events apply to all humans, manages daily routines.

FIFTH YEAR—Mature motor control, hops, skips, speaks clearly, tells long stories, sure of self, often follows socially acceptable behavior.

SIXTH YEAR—Child now center of own universe, separating, relationship with mother is ambivalent, behavior difficult, insecure, thinks mother doesn't love him, interested in being good, friends are important, still interested in magic and death.

SEVENTH YEAR—Lives in a world of thought, worrier, fearful, wants to be perfect. Has ethical standards, fair, tries to tell the truth, some abstract thought, collector, easier relationship with mother, home and family, developing awareness of others.

EIGHTH YEAR—More separation from mother, dependent and possessive of her, argues with her, relates to others more easily than previously, may have best friend, more outgoing, language is coming into its own, explores new territory, hard on himself for mistakes, thinks in terms of right and wrong, often can listen to reason, loves to play children's games of all kinds.

NINTH YEAR—Pivotal year, tremendous individual differences at this age, more independent, likes to be given responsibility, can focus, notices details, emotions more subtle, good age for improving academic skills, can make self do hard or unpleasant things, strong willpower, thinks ahead, new awareness of self and others, hoards, further conscience development, likes to talk things over, developing interest in present and future, disgust with opposite sex, believes less in magic.

PREADOLESCENCE: (10,11,12)—Hormonal changes taking place in body which will lead to puberty, increase in physical activity, appetite, and physical growth, much energy put into awareness or denial of coming puberty.

PUBERTY: THE BEGINNING OF ADOLESCENCE—Wide variation in ways individuals cope. Menstruation in girls, erection, ejaculation and nocturnal emissions in boys, intense preoccupation with body changes.

EARLY ADOLESCENCE: DIVIDED INTO TWO MAJOR PHASES. IN BOTH PHASES ALTERNATING PERIODS OF INTEGRATED BEHAVIOR WITH MORE UNRELIABLE BEHAVIOR—First phase begins with increase in instinctual drives. Strong sexual and aggressive impulses, emotional equilibrium upset, intense activity required to achieve any degree of balance or avoid being emotionally overwhelmed, tantrums and outbursts last until middle teens. Crushes on adults, importance of peer group's values, including music, dress, jargon, telephone, masturbation.

LATE ADOLESCENCE—Better ability to function, improved stabilization of underlying biological processes, fear and panic of beginning puberty recedes, more logic and rational argument used. Youngster usually shifts dependency needs from parent to boyfriend or girlfriend. Begins to reason and debate on philosophical issues, more open to psychotherapy, more self-observation and self—evaluation, greater psychological stability, some disequilibrium continues.

END OF ADOLESCENCE—Comes when psychological disequilibrium is replaced by a relatively stable equilibrium, whether it is adaptive or maladaptive.

POST ADOLESCENCE—Often goes through extreme phase-grows beard, experiments with hair, drugs, alcohol, lives in and out of friends' homes, uneven school performance, casual about money, borrows from one another and takes from parents, becomes involved in protest movements, often idealistic, feelings of alienation, need for individuality, may not be ready to enter adult world, values and standards solidifying, struggle between impulse and conscience development, choice of occupation central in search for identity.

RESOLUTION OF ADOLESCENCE—Achievement of independence and, firm identity, and ability to establish ways of managing instinctual drives which allows one to maintain a stable mental and emotional equilibrium.

Graphics by
Little Heart Inc.

APPENDIX A

OPTIMIZING ATTACHMENT BETWEEN CHILD AND PARENT

PURPOSE OF ATTACHMENT:
To build trust
To provide a sense of security
To aid in the development of conscience, sense of identity, feelings of mastery, control and self-worth.
To enhance the ability to socialize
To develop the ability to accept love and to feel love for another

PRINCIPLES OF ATTACHMENT:

- Parents must be attuned to their child's natural schedule for sleep, feeding and play. There have already been many unpreventable frustrations that this child has encountered, and there will continue to be others. These are children who may not trust that their needs will be met so they are have a harder time dealing with disappointments and delays. By focusing on the baby's needs and wants rather than on the maintenance of an imposed schedule, additional frustrations may be minimized. Therefore, parental responses must be immediate and appropriate.

- Parents should be attuned to the child's emotions. The child may be grieving over the loss of an earlier caregiver. Allow him time to mourn and be there to help him deal with the loss. It is important at this time that his emotions be soothed. He should be held, cradled and sung to but not denied opportunities to feel his sadness.

- Maximize the time spent together. This adopted child is not a child who should be left with babysitters or other surrogates. He needs consistent care from the primary caregiver who must also do all of the feeding, bathing, changing and other activities that facilitate bonding.

- There should be consistency of attitude and performance from the mother. A child should be able to trust that routines and responses will be consistent. Feeding, napping, bedtime should be on a regular schedule and emotional responses should also be predictable.

- The mother must provide the model for a range of facial expressions such as smiling and frowning and all of the expressions in between. She should maintain eye contact when tending her child so that he will mimic her behaviors and maintain a feeling of being connected.

- Close physical contact with the child must be maintained so that he feels as if he is almost an extension of the mother. Hold the child whenever you can, rock him, cuddle him and encourage him to touch your face and hair. If you can't always hold him, keep him in the same room. This will encourage a sense of security and comfort, especially if he was not held enough before he joined your family. Keep him on a bottle longer than is usual and use the opportunity to hold him even more. Bathe with him. Such activities as hand feeding while holding the child, rather than propping a bottle, rocking, hugging, tickling, singing, massaging and engaging in playful behavior while maintaining eye and physical contact are essential. As he gets older and is toddling and walking around allow him to be your shadow to maintain that closeness.

- Closely monitor your child's performance by staying with him or encouraging him to check in frequently with you. As he grows older, it is important to carefully supervise his chores and homework. He needs you to see that work is done and done to some previously established standard. Providing opportunities for success will help build feelings of mastery and accomplishment. Limit opportunities for your child to make poor decisions which affect his sense of security and self-worth and thus jeopardize the attachment. A child who feels good about himself feels connected to others.

- Your child's time should be structured during the day so that there are many opportunities to engage in meaningful activities and idle time is minimized.

- Demonstrate affection regardless of your child's responses to that affection. He needs to be held and kissed and stroked even if he rejects these demonstrations of love.

- Nurture a happy and loving nature through shared play and modeling playful behavior. Happy surprises, mystery activities, silly moments are wonderful for developing this attitude. Toys and objects that encourage attachments should be readily available.

- Be aware of your child's need to behave as if at a younger age and allow him time to be there. If he wants to talk "baby talk" or crawl when he can walk, allow him opportunities to regress. Conversely, allow opportunities for him to play out more mature roles.

- Articulate your child's conscience until his sense of morality is strongly developed. Simple conversations about the relationship between cause and effect and the consequences of alternative actions are important for these children.

- Avoid control battles. State what has to be done or what is expected and don't be diverted by side issues. If discipline is necessary, follow up with a time for affection and reassurance to avoid leaving the child with feelings of shame and worthlessness which will weaken the attachment. Do not isolate your child with "time outs" alone in his room. This will only increase his feelings of separateness. Have the child do his thinking time near you so that he will feel safe and the bond will be reinforced even in difficult times.

- Go at the child's pace in order not to overwhelm her. Be aware that occasionally the child must withdraw and have space in order to stay balanced. While developing attachment, it will be necessary for the major caretakers to keep in mind the ultimate goal and inch her toward attachment rather than insisting on it.

*** The word "mother" is used here to represent the primary bonding object in the attachment relationship.

Appendix B
SELECTING A THERAPIST

- Be aware that most therapists have neither the training nor experience to deal with issues of attachment.

- Resist the temptation to stop therapy when things seem to be getting better. Untreated attachment problems can lead to the development of unhealthy behavioral problems which become harder to treat in later years.

- Choose a therapist who is familiar with the developmental implications of adoption and childhood attachment.

- Select a therapist who is willing to communicate with you on a continuing basis.

SOURCES FOR REFERRAL:

Word of mouth with other adoptive parents
Other therapists
Schools-Guidance Counselors, Psychologists, Social Workers
Evaluators: Educational, Psychoeducational, and Homestudy
Pediatricians
Neurologists
Educational Remediators
CHADD
Support groups focused on ADD or learning disabilities

INFORMATION TO PROVIDE FOR THERAPIST:

- Age at time of adoption

- Early background information-birthparents, prenatal care, medical and genetic information, substance use, early child rearing conditions

- Developments and changes after child is brought home

- Meeting of developmental milestones from birth to time therapy is begun (sitting up, giving up bottle, crawling, talking, walking etc.)

QUESTIONS TO ASK:

- Does the therapist appear to be open minded, creative, a good listener and observer and willing to learn new techniques?

- How will the child be assessed? This process may take quite a while and can not be done in one session.

- Does the therapist understand the unique issues related to adoption such as bonding, attachment, the effects of changing caregivers?

- Does the therapist have access to other resources such as educational attorneys and consultants?

- Is the therapist willing to treat the problem in a way that is appropriate for the age of the child? In the early years therapy may focus on parenting skills required for the child with attachment disorders since the early interaction between parent and child is critical. As the child matures, therapy will possibly involve direct therapy between the child and the therapist.

- Does the therapist have an understanding of the behavioral implications related to ADD and learning disabilities and the ability to diagnose these conditions or refer for diagnosis?

- Is the therapist capable of assessing an older child for attachment issues which have not been recognized in younger years?

  In selecting the best therapist it is important that you have confidence in your ability to take the lead by asking the questions that are important to you and your family. You know your child better than anyone else, and it will be your responsibility to teach the professional about your child. This is key to making an accurate evaluation and developing a plan for treatment.

APPENDIX C
ADDITIONAL RESOURCES

When problems become apparent it is not always easy to seek help. The following are a list of sources that you might consult at such a time.

Know what you are up against in terms of learning disabilities, substance abuse and your rights as a parent.

CHILD DEVELOPMENT CENTERS
CHILD STUDY CENTERS
EDUCATIONAL ATTORNEYS
EDUCATIONAL CONSULTANTS
LEARNING DISABILITIES ASSOCIATION
LOCAL STUDENT ADVOCACY GROUPS
MENTAL HEALTH ASSOCIATIONS
ORTON DYSLEXIA SOCIETY

WEB SITES:

www.bgcenter.com: Center for Cognitive-Development Assessment and Remediation (BG Center)—psychoeducational services for internationally adopted children preschool and school age.

www.boardingschoolreview.com: directory, compares schools using several criteria, lists fairs and events.

www.drugprevention.net: how to recognize drug use

www.educationalconsultring.org: lists educational consultants by state and schools

www.educationalconsulting.org: website for the Independent Educational Consulting Assn. provides professional information about consultants, schools, uses thorough evaluation to direct parents and professionals.

www.ldaamerica.org: information and resources for parents of children with a variety of learning disabilities.

www.marthawelch.com: family treatment therapy and training for families with children suffering from behavioral and developmental disorders including Reactive Attachment Disorder.

www.natsap.org: *National Association of Therapeutic Schools and Programs, Program Directory*, how to choose a program, asking the right question, varied articles.

www.petersons.com: *Directory Of Private Secondary Schools*, now available on the website, includes specific schools, varied programs, statistics, descriptions and much more

www.strugglingteens.com: broad range of information for parents of troubled teenagers including variety of programs and sites to locate youth transport companies.

www.suite101.com: adoption related articles

www.tapestrybooks.com: bookseller specializes in adoption related issues

wrightslaw.com: up to date information about school advocacy for children with special needs, state and federal law, strategies etc.

SUPPORT GROUPS:

AA-Alcoholic Anonymous

CHADD-Children and Adults with Attention Deficit Hyperactivity Disorder

NACAC-North American Council on Adoptable Children-source for adoption support groups.

ALANON-for families of alcoholics

ALATEEN—for teenagers with substance abuse problems

NARCOTICS ANONYMOUS

FAMILIES ANONYMOUS—help for the families of children with substance and behavioral issues.

DIRECTORIES AND OTHER BOOKS:

The Connected Child, Karyn B. Purvis PhD, David R. Cross PhD and Wendt Lyons Sunshine-how to parent adopted children emphasizing attachment concepts.

The Face In The Mirror: Teenagers And Adoption, Marion Crook-good teenage fiction.

The Parent Empowerment Handbook 2004/2005-up to date information on 100+ private therapeutic, emotional growth, LD, wilderness schools available at amazon.com.

A Tribe Apart, Patricia Hersch-cultural influences on teenagers.

Toddler Adoption: The Weaver's Craft, Mary Hopkins-Best

Peterson's Directory Of Private Secondary Schools

Teens In Turmoil, Carol Maxym, and Leslie York-Getting help for troubled teens, includes good resources among all of its helpful information.

When Love Is Not Enough, Nancy Thomas—Parental strategies for nurturing and providing structure for a child with RAD.

From Emotions To Advocacy: The Special Education Survival Guide, Pam and Peter Wright-available through website wrightslaw.com—a must for people dealing with the public school system, legal issues, tactics, advocacy and much more

EDUCATIONAL PROGRAMS:

- Emotional growth-behavioral: Based on developing independence, reliability, moral and ethical values. Teaches student to take responsibility for oneself and others and develop goals for excellence.

- Learning Disabilities: Specifically devoted to student who has been diagnosed with learning disabilities. Teaches structure and organization and helps student gain confidence and independence in study habits and skills and become a successful and functioning learner.

- Therapeutic: In patient and out patient programs designed to work with children and teens who have been diagnosed with psychological disorders and who in most cases have experienced an emotional crisis that requires treatment.

- Wilderness: Aimed at teaching survival skills and development of personal strengths and self-reliance. Most often used to teach adolescents who have not been able to function in their home community due to inability to follow rules, or to rely on their inner strengths and inner structure which includes a value system. Requires a dramatic change in setting and rigid adherence to adult expectations.

- Drug and Alcohol Rehabilitation: Assess and treat youngsters with substance abuse problems. Can be residential or nonresidential.

BIBLIOGRAPHY

Ames, Louise Bates Ph.D and Carol Chase Haber. Gesell Institute of Human Development. *Your Eight-Year Old, Lively and Outgoing.* New York: Dell Publishing. 1989.

Ames, Louise Bates Ph.D. and Carol Chase Haber. Gesell Institute of Human Development. *Your Nine-Year Old, Thoughtful and Mysterious.* New York: Dell Publishing. 1991.

Ames, Louise Bates Ph.D and Carol Chase Haber. Gesell Institute of Human Development. *Your Seven-Year Old, Life in a Minor Key.* New York: Delacorte Press. 1985.

Ames, Louise Bates Ph.D and Frances L. Ilg. Gesell Institute of Human Development. *Your Six-Year Old, Defiant but Loving.* New York: Dell Publishing. 1979.

Ames, Louise Bates Ph.D and Frances L. Ilg and Sidney N. Baker M.D. Gesell Institute of Human Development. *Your Ten to Fourteen-Year Old.* New York: Dell Publishing.1956.

Bowlby, John. *Attachment.* New York: Basic Books, Inc. 1969.

Blanck, Gertrude and Rubin Blanck. *Ego Psychology I: Theory and Practice.* New York: Columbia University Press.1974

Brazelton, T. Berry and Bertrand G. Cramer M.D. *The Earliest Relationship.* Cambridge, MA: Perseus Book.1990.

Brazelton. T. Berry, M.D. *On Becoming a Family.* New York: Dell Publishing.1992.

Brodzinsky, David M. Ph.D. and Marshall D. Schechter M.D. and Robin Marantz Henig. *Being Adopted: The Lifelong Search for Self.* New York: Anchor Books. 1993.

Cline, Foster. W. M.D. and Cathy Helding. *Can This Child Be Saved?* Franksville, WI: World Enterprises. 1999.

The Committee on Adolescence, Group for the Advancement Psychiatry. *Normal Adolescence.* New York: Charles Scribner's Sons. 1968.

Erikson, Erik H. *Identity Youth and Crisis.* New York: W.W. Norton & Company Inc. 1968.

Fraiberg, Selma. *Clinical Studies in Infant Mental Health: The First Years of Life.* New York: Basic Books, Inc. 1980.

Freud, Anna. *The Writings of Anna Freud Vol. VI 1965: Normality and Pathology in Childhood: Assessments of Development.* International Universities Press, Inc. New York. 1965.

Gesell, Arnold M.D. *The First Five Years of Life.* New York: Harper & Brothers Publishers. 1989.

Gould, Joseph W. *Character First.* Bath, Maine: The Hyde Foundation.1993.

Gray, Deborah D. *Attaching in Adoption Practical Tools for Today's Parents.* Indianapolis, Indiana: Perspectives Press, Inc. 2002.

Greenacre, Phyllis. "The Childhood of the Artist: Libidinal Phase Development and Giftedness." *The Psychoanalytic Study of the Child.* New York: International Universities Press. 1957.

Hughes, Daniel A. *Building the Bonds of Attachment.* New Jersey: Jason Aronsin Inc. 1998.

James, Beverly. *Handbook for Treatment of Attachment-Trauma Problemsin Children.* New York: The Tree Press. 1994.

Kaplan, Louise J. PhD. *Oneness and Separateness: From Infant To Individual.* New York: Simon and Schuster. 1978.

Koplewicz, Harold S. PhD. *It's Nobody's Fault.* New York: Random House (Times Books). 1996.

Kirk, H. David. *Shared Fate: A Theory and Method of Adoptive Relationships*. Port Angeles, Washington: Ben Simon Publications. 1984

Levy, Terry M. and Michael Orlans. *Attachment, Trauma and Healing*. Washington D.C. CWLA Press. 1998.

Lewis, Thomas, M.D. Amini, Fari, M.D. and Lannon Richard, M.D.. *A General Theory of Love*. New York: Vintage Books. 2000.

Loux, Ann Kimble. *The Limits of Hope*. USA: The University Press of Virginia. 1977.

Magid, Dr. Ken and Carole A. *High Risk*. New York: Bantam Books. 1987.

Mahler, Margaret S. and Fred Pine and Anni Bergman. *The Psychological Birth of the Human Infant*. New York: Basic Books. 1975.

Mash, Eric J. and Russell A. Barkley. *Treatment of Childhood Disorders*. New York. The Guildford Press. 1989.

McKelvey, Carole MA, Editor. *Give Them Roots, Then Let Them Fly*. The Attachment Center at Evergreen, Inc. USA. Morris Publishing. 1995.

Melina, Lois Ruskai. *Making Sense of Adoption A Parent Guide*. New York: Harper & Row, Publishers. 1989.

Neubauer. Peter B. M.D. and Alexander Neubauer. *Nature's Thumbprint: The New Genetics of Personality*. New York. Columbia University Press. 1996.

Peterson, Janelle. *Can Do! Compendium on Post-Legal Adoption Service*. Denver, Colorado. Loving Homes, Inc. 1998.

Schwebel, Milton and Jane Rath (Eds.). *Piaget in the Classroom. New York*. Basic Books Inc. Publications. 1973.

Shilts, Donna. *Love is a Start*. Portland, Oregon: Look Again Publishing.1999.

Spitz, Rene A. *The First Year of Life: A Psychoanalytic Study of Normal and Deviant Development of Object Relations*. New York: International Universities Press, Inc. 1965.

Spitz, Rene A. *No & Yes: On the Genesis of Human Communication.* New York: International Universities Press, Inc. 1957.

Verrier, Nancy Newton. *The Primal Wound.* Baltimore, MD. Gateway Press, Inc. 1999.

Wade, Nicholas. November 22, 2005. "Exploring a Hormone for Caring." NY Times page F5.

Weil, John Leopold, M.D. *Early Deprivation of Empathetic Care.* Madison, Connecticut. International Universities Press. 1992

Young, J.Z. *Programs of the Brain.* Oxford: Oxford University Press. 1968.

ABOUT THE AUTHORS

Jean Roe Mauro

Early in her career, Jean Roe Mauro, LCSW realized that her primary professional interest was in the health and welfare of children. A career in social work gave her the opportunity to pursue this field in depth. Her training included a certificate in child psychotherapy and community mental health practice from the Madeleine Borg Child Guidance Institute of the Jewish Board of Guardians, a children's agency in New York City. She subsequently studied at the Blanck Institute for the Study of Psychoanalytic Psychotherapy also in New York City.

As a psychotherapist Jean worked and supervised in agencies across the country that specialized in foster care, residential treatment, adoptive services and child therapy. These agencies serve babies, birthmothers and adoptive families. Included among those agencies are The Child Welfare Unit in Oklahoma City, Hope Cottage-Children's Bureau in Dallas, The Children's Center in Atlanta, Vanderbilt Hospital Children's Unit in Nashville, Hawthorne Cedar Knolls Residential Treatment Center of the Jewish board of Guardians, and Windward School in White Plains. She has also worked extensively with children and adults with learning disabilities and ADD.

Jean has been an active member, conference speaker and workshop facilitator for The Adoptive Parents Committee in the New York area. An adoptive parent herself, she has intimate knowledge of the subject and its influence on child development. Through her extensive research, Jean has been able to synthesize the work of pioneers and current researchers in the field of child development and present this information in a straightforward and easily understandable manner.

A psychotherapist in private practice in White Plains, NY for many years, Jean specializes in child, adolescent and family therapy with an emphasis on adoption.

Sara-Jane Hardman

Sara-Jane Hardman has lived in the New York area all her life. For many years she was an English teacher and administrator in the New York City School system. During her career she worked with children from many backgrounds with varied histories and family stories. These included youngsters representing a range of developmental stages, each with his unique personality and learning style. As an adoptive parent and adoption advocate, she was President of the Adoptive Parents Committee in Westchester/Rockland counties where she ran workshops for adoptive families and immersed herself in adoption-related issues. Today she is president of the Lifetime Learning Institute at Bard College in Annandale-on-Hudson, New York.

The authors' previous writings can be viewed on line at the adoptionarticles/directory.com. They are currently preparing a twenty hour on-line parenting course for the BG Center for Cognitive-Developmental Assessment and Remediation in Nanuet, NY.

INDEX

978-0-595-46194-3
0-595-46194-8

Printed in the United States
206440BV00005B/28-36/A